Beyond the Alps

Robert M. Coates

Beyond the Alps

A SUMMER IN THE ITALIAN HILL TOWNS

Pictures by Astrid Peters Coates

William Sloane Associates
New York, 1961

TO LAURENCE—*Who Helped a Lot*

Contents

Outpost of Empire

The last time I came into Italy from France, which was also the first time I did it by car, was by way of the Great St. Bernard Pass. The route went past the famous Hospice, a rather barren set of buildings on the whole, gaunt but massive, and at some 8,170 feet supposedly the highest human habitation of any consequence in all Europe, and then down along the valley of the Buthier River to the edge of the plains of the Piedmont, over six thousand feet below. The road is steep and winding and for the most part heavily forested, but on the way there are glimpses to be had of some of the highest peaks in the Alps, from Mont Dolent to the south almost all the way up to the Matterhorn, in the north.

This time, it was over the Little St. Bernard, somewhat farther south of the other and about one thousand feet lower, and on the whole I liked it better. There were three of us in the party, my wife, myself, and our old friend Laurence Vail, who has lived, so to speak, between France and Italy most of his life. He is an artist himself; and his father, an artist too, was one of those fortunate turn-of-the-century expatriates who could afford to live in Paris and spend their winters in

Italy, taking the family along. One of the luckiest things about the whole trip, for me, was that he was able to make a good part of it with us.

From the Little St. Bernard, the road down into Italy again follows a mountain stream, this one called the Dora Baltea, and is equally precipitous. But perhaps because the valley is more enclosed the feeling is more intimate; if, apart from some sudden, startling glimpses of Mont Blanc, standing huge and white in the distance, there are few "big" views to be had there are dozens of smaller ones, and they are the more enchanting for the swiftness with which they pass.

One of the most remarkable things about the mountains of the Alps, I think, is the smoothness of the progression from the barrenness of the heights to the fertility of the populated plains below. To the American, accustomed to thinking in terms of the Rockies, the idea of a really big mountain carries with it an implication of solitude and relative inaccessibility: a big mountain, to most of us, is something seen from afar, set down in a waste of its own and arrived at only by a long and difficult journey by jeep or by mule pack. Things are different in the Alps, for there the great peaks spring directly from the farm land, and the transition from one to the other is gradual.

Though the time was mid-May, the Little St. Bernard had only recently been opened (all the higher passes, of course, were still closed, blocked by snow, as they had been throughout the winter) and our car was among the first to cross it. Climbing up the French side, we had been in snow country for some time, and at the summit the road ran through drifts that were occasionally considerably higher than the roof of the car. As we dropped down into Italy, it was interesting to see how smooth and almost imperceptible the change was.

The snow went first, of course, tailing off into streaks and then into patches, and lodged first among huge, bare buttresses of rock and then among scrub pines, firs and larches.

Farther down, the pines grew larger, and the birches and other of the hardier deciduous trees crept in among them; grass appeared among the shoulders of rock, and then the rock raveled off into scattered snow-wrinkled boulders, lying here and there in what was beginning to be pasture land; one saw too, now and then in the fields, little, low-roofed, battered-looking but still sturdy structures, built of stone, logs and stucco all thrown together, which would serve as shelters for the farmers' cattle when they were brought up for summer pasture.

By now, little settlements had begun to appear, seen first, as the road angled down from above, as a patchwork pattern of differently colored, weather-beaten tile roofs; and then, after a switchback curve, as a huddle of gaunt façades, with a tiny caffè and a store or two grouped around a small, paved piazza, and a woman, perhaps, drawing a pitcher of water from the communal fountain or pump in the middle, and turning her head to look casually at the car as it passed.

By now, too, the terraced farming had begun. The Piedmont is a great wine-growing region. Both the Barberas and the less well-known but subtler Barolo wines come from there, and though their main production is on the plains farther south we passed acres and acres of land that had been planted to vines in the last, still precipitous stages of our descent. The fields were terraced, of course, and to me there is always something amazing in the assiduity with which even the steepest of these slopes have been brought under cultivation. It's a testimony both to the value of arable land in these overpopulated areas and to the ageless patience and industry of man, for the carrying and cutting and laying-up of the stones alone must have, in the aggregate, taken centuries—and so not have been done solely for the profit of one man but for his followers and descendants; in a sense, for the land itself.

Yet here the terraces stand, and they are beautiful in their way: the land cut back and tiered step by step, following the contours, and each tier leveled off and stoned up in strips until in the end a whole hillside will present the look of a giant, green, fertile staircase—or, if you will, a vineyard partially upended.

From then on, the trip down is just a matter of bigger farms and larger villages, the road less steep and winding and with more activity on it until—a scant twenty miles and around six thousand feet lower than the snow fields above, but in the gentlest and most continuous of transitions—one comes out on the relatively flat lands below.

To be sure, there are easier ways of getting into Italy from France by car than by either of these mountain passes. One can go by the coast road through Genoa and down along the old Roman Via Aurelia (now a busy truck route) or, for that matter, by way of the Simplon Tunnel, where the automobiles are loaded onto a flatcar and their occupants ride in an antiquated railway carriage ahead: the whole trip takes only an hour or so. Whichever of the St. Bernard routes one takes, however, the road leads to the town of Aosta, for Aosta lies at the confluence of the Dora Baltea and Buthier rivers, and I chose the Aosta way because from even what little I had seen of it on my previous trip the town, little known and in many ways unimpressive as it is, had fascinated me. Although it is always dangerous to try to recapture first impressions, in this case, happily, I found it just as charming in its own quiet, unpretentious way as I had before.

I find it a little difficult to define the attraction it has for me. Certainly, it has none of the beguiling qualities one associates with the more famous towns farther south. Though it lies on a little plateau of its own, it is a mountain town pure and simple, with all that mixture of easy-goingness and independence that goes with it.

There are high peaks pretty much all around it—some of

them, like Grivolo and the Gran Paradiso, Fallière and Monte Emilius, well known to mountain climbers. All are ten to twelve thousand feet high and are snow-covered or snow-capped according to the season. They are major peaks, and whether one thinks of climbing them or not they dominate the town, rising above the roofs in almost every direction one looks and isolating it from the less rugged regions farther down.

Perhaps because of Aosta's isolation, no great painters or sculptors visited it,* or they left no works there if they did, and so what importance the town has as a repository of the arts is infinitesimal. A small civic museum has been set up hopefully in a building on the via de Sales, a side street not far from the main square, but its contents are mainly of local or archaeological interest and the attendance slim. The guidebooks give Aosta only a paragraph or two, and although there are hopes that the new Mont Blanc Vehicular Tunnel, now under construction, will eventually bring more tourists to the town, it is now little visited.

Indeed, what antiquities it has are mostly Roman, and it occurs to me that this fact may lie somewhere at the root of its attraction for me. Thin and meager as its history is in one sense, it is certainly lengthy and, in much the same way that I used the word in describing its Alpine approaches, continuous.

It was a garrison town in the days of the Empire, and in a way it remains one, for despite the changes and overgrowths that have occurred in the centuries between, the town is still, in its basic outlines, purely Roman: the outer walls, or what now is left of them, laid out foursquare, and the main streets inside them, for all the interweaving of alleys and byways

* I'm speaking here of the men of the Italian Renaissance. English artists on the Grand Tour, with their taste for the ruggedly picturesque, passed by there in some numbers, and Turner, in particular, made some striking watercolor studies of the mountains and valleys round-about.

that have since been superposed upon them, still preserving
that strict rectangularity that the Romans delighted in.

Above all, its very small size and compactness give it
value. Rome, in the archaeological sense, isn't Rome any
more. Far too much has happened there through the centuries for one to be able to get much idea of what it was
really like in the days of the Empire. In Aosta, the past is
clearer. The part it played in the great strategy of Imperial
developments may have been small indeed—roughly comparable, say, to that of Fort Laramie or any other outpost town
in the conquest of the West—but that only makes one's idea
of the way of life as it went on in it the easier of compre-
hension.

At any rate, I found it a delightful place to wander in. As
I've said, its history is meager, and although its position at
the approaches to two of the main Alpine passes must
always have given it a certain strategic importance, it was not
until around the last quarter of the first century before Christ,
rather late in the expansionist phase of the Empire, that the
Romans turned their attention to it.

At that time, it was the headquarters of a mountain tribe
called the Selassi, and the Selassi, until progress caught up
with them, seem to have had things pretty much their own
way in the region. In fact, they might be said to have had
things both ways, going and coming. They were miners on
the one hand and bandits on the other—producing, in their
first capacity, iron and, according to some accounts, gold from
secret sources in the mountains and selling these to the more
peaceable people of the plains; and then, like as not, in their
second role, waylaying and robbing their customers on the
trails below!

In their own good time, however, the Romans put a stop
to such nonsense. The fact was that by then, if the Empire
was to continue its expansion beyond the Alps, the passes
and their approaches had to be secured; and in the year

25 B.C., a force of some three thousand Praetorian Guards, under the general Varro Murena, marched up, flushed the tribesmen out and destroyed them. (They flushed them out literally too, incidentally, for it appears that the Selassi had their habitations mainly in caves; and the Romans, by damming the rivers and backing up the waters, succeeded in flooding their caves and either drowning them or driving them out into the open, where of course they could make mincemeat of them. The Romans were, first and foremost, engineers.)

It must have been a fairly bloodless campaign, on the Roman side at least, for Pliny, that indefatigable chronicler, scarcely mentions it. But easy though the conquest was, the occupation was thorough; and the outpost town that was erected to house the three thousand Praetorians—run up in the space of a year, incidentally, and called originally Augusta Praetoria Salassorum; since reduced, by the wildest of telegraphese, to Aosta—even now has the appearance of having been a fairly formidable stronghold.

The late Romans cheated outrageously in their construction. Always reaching for massiveness of appearance, they often cored their walls with rubble,* saving the fine facing-stone for the outer surfaces; and by now, with the passing of centuries—plus, no doubt, some amiable pilfering on the part of later builders—the facing of the fortifications as well as that of the other contemporary structures has largely disappeared.

* It was a device that paid off handsomely, however, for the Romans speedily discovered that the rock they were using for fill, mainly volcanic in origin, made a particularly durable amalgam when mixed with crushed lime and water: in effect, concrete. After that, there was no stopping them, and such soaring structures resulted as the walls and arches of the great Baths of Caracalla, Diocletian and so on—still, I'm told, mystifying to modern builders in view of the fact that they were put up, apparently, without any reinforcement.

Their walls too, by the same twin processes of erosion, have shrunk in height from an original twenty-odd feet to a wavering half of that. Yet they still carry a feeling of the formidable about them, and the one gate that remains in recognizable shape, the Porta Pretoria—the one, no doubt, from which the troops sallied forth to patrol the countryside —is a double gate, really, with enough room between its twin portals to house a considerable body of guards and sentries.

Just beyond, on the road leading out of town and spanning it, is a triumphal arch dedicated to the Emperor Augustus, in whose reign the conquest was made. There is no record that I know of that Augustus ever visited Aosta. He was probably far too busy at the moment with matters relating to the East to have time for that. But one gets the impression that the Romans could run up a triumphal arch as readily as we can construct a cloverleaf overpass. It was one of their best accomplishments, and the Aostan arch may have been put there for no other reason than to impress the natives.

Just inside the gate, there are the ruins of a Roman theater (after all, like soldiers on faraway posts in any era, the Praetorians had to be amused) and these, though again a trifle small by Imperial standards, are nevertheless impressive and also, as far as their plan goes, complete.

The high, slablike stone structure which served as a permanent backdrop is beautifully proportioned. It is pierced with three tiers of arched fenestrations to relieve its weight and lend grace to it; and the semicircular stage, with its underground passageways which served as entrances and exits, together with the concentric rings of stone seats in front of it, are all neatly ordered and well preserved. The area around it has been turned, in the most casual fashion, into a public park; when I was there it was pleasantly alive with people strolling, while at the theater itself a group of workmen were laying a temporary flooring on top of the ancient Roman stone-flagged one, to serve as a stage for a choral festival to be held the following Sunday. But for all that, it was still easy enough to imagine a Roman equivalent of a USO troupe dancing out on the stage to delight a packed audience of Roman soldiery.

There is not a great deal of history that is pertinent to us after the Roman era, in Aosta. Napoleon passed through there in 1800—on his way, as it developed, to the battle of Marengo, decisive against the Austrians. He was welcomed in Aosta, the whole township turning out to do him honor, though he met with resistance on his way down the valley, farther on. (Hannibal, incidentally, had passed through earlier, in 216 A.D., on *his* way to the battle of Lake Trasimeno, almost equally decisive against the Romans.) In medieval times, Aosta's position controlling the cisalpine approaches to the two passes gave it commanding military importance, and the Counts, later Dukes, of Aosta were powerful and respected personages indeed, dealing for a time on equal terms with the Kings of France and England.*

Later, in the endless shuttlings of possessions and power in the Renaissance and the Middle Ages, it was absorbed by the Dukes of Savoy, whose holdings then straddled the Alps. Since Victor Emmanuel, who became the first King of Italy after the unification of 1861, was of that line, it became a part of the Royal House of Italy, with the title of Duke of Aosta and Savoy an appanage of the family. Ironically, as a part of the price that made unification possible, Italy had to cede to France the transalpine side of Savoy, including

* The Italian liner *Conte Verde* was named after one of the Counts of Aosta, Amadeus VI. He was called the "Green Count" because he always wore that color in jousting. Another vessel, the *Biancamano*, or "White Hand" was named after his father. Both, apparently, were just and pacific men, for their times, and the Green Count, historically, is credited with being the first ruler to provide free legal aid to his poorer subjects appearing in his courts. You can see why I like Aosta.

Nice—though not Aosta. Aosta and its surrounding territory, called the Val d'Aosta, has had a quasi-autonomous status, as a province, or county, ever since.

So much for capsule history, and I have made it brief because surprisingly little of this part of Aosta's past remains to color the atmosphere of the town today. Here and there, along the original Roman walls, small towers have been added, mostly dating from the twelfth or thirteenth century. The Romans, curiously, rarely included turreting in their fortifications. They were sappers primarily, preferring to undermine the towers of their enemies. But in the brawling Middle Ages the steep, narrow gorges of the Dora Baltea, as it runs down the Val d'Aosta, south of the town, seem to have looked more attractive to the military-minded; and it is there, at places like Nus, Bard (so strong that even Napoleon succeeded in taking it only at night, by surprise attack), Issogne and so on, that one finds the really important medieval strongholds, perched grim-walled and battlemented, but now abandoned, on the rocky spurs overlooking and commanding the river.

Otherwise, the main charm of Aosta is its casualness. In a sense, the town has overflowed its past, absorbing it in the process; and with that marvelous capacity the Italians have for adapting past structures to present needs, the old walls have been put to the wildest variety of uses—serving here to buttress one side of a tiny Gothic convent and there as the foundation for a fifteenth-century dwelling, while a bit farther on, where they close off the end of a garden, they have been made to serve as the backing for a row of fruit trees, pleached.

So they thread through the life of the town, while elsewhere, by one of those tit-for-tat sequences that are common in history, the Cattedrale, or main church of the town—a grandiose but not particularly beautiful structure, heavily Ro-

manesque in style, with an overlay of late Renaissance restoration, including queer conical steeples on the solid old,
square, neo-Gothic towers—has been superposed on a section
of the Roman forum, where a pagan temple to Diana was
located; and the temple, according to tradition, was built on
the still more pagan site of a sacrificial altar of the Selassi.
(By the same token, the Augustan arch now sports a large
and extremely handsome carved wooden Crucifixion, dating
from around the twelfth century, suspended under the vaulting.)

Tomasso XI, Count of Savoy, is buried in the Cathedral,
in a grim but imposing thirteenth-century tomb, and the mosaic pavement in the nave is attractive. But the main pride of
the town, ecclesiastically, is its Sant'Anselmo, who was born
there in 1033 and went on, via France, to become Archbishop
of Canterbury—where he had the dangerous task of uphold-
ing the primacy of the Pope against the power of the English
Crown itself.

One of the medieval towers, the Torre dei Balivi, or "Bail-
iffs' Tower," has been converted, with a sort of wry appro-
priateness, into a *carcere giudiziere,* or town jail. The Torre
del Lebbroso, or "Leper's Tower," is so named because of an
ancient, murky legend about a mysterious leper who was put
there to die; later on, it gained a certain renown as having
been the inspiration of a once extremely popular, but now
forgotten Gothic tale by the eighteenth-century novelist, Xa-
vier de Maistre. When I was there, a family of ragpickers
had made the ruin their warehouse; it was spring, and around
it a small grove of cherry trees was in bloom.

The Tour Bramafam is the most pretentious. (No "*Torre,*"
this time: the whole Val d'Aosta is incurably bilingual in its
nomenclature, switching capriciously from Italian to French
and back again without apparent reason.) A big, round elev-
enth-century edifice, once the keep of a vanished castle, it
sits now in a small but well tended, grassy park space, re-

served for children—another sign of the homely easy-goingness of the town. Grouped around a little piazza out by the Augustan arch, are a twelfth-century bell tower; an early Romanesque, and very beautiful, cloister; and the Collegiate Church of Sant'Orso, or Ursula, most of which dates from the late fifteenth century. Plus a huge and venerable, wide-branching lime tree, the whole forms, by one of those happy conjunctions which seem to arise independently of architectural styles and sequences, one of the most charming scenes imaginable. (As another example of time's casualness in Aosta, a little trattoria, or tavern, fits quite comfortably into a Roman guardhouse between the portals of the Porta Pretoria, while just outside the Gate a chair-caner, at the time I was there, had set up his establishment in the open air. He was a short, chunky fellow in a bright-red beret, always whistling, and the work he was doing looked pretty expert, too.)

In another sense, though, the town has come back to its own beginnings. It is still, after all the centuries, a garrison town in the real sense, for a considerable number of Alpine troops are quartered there. Most of them are new recruits, there for training; one sees them, evenings, looking rather awkward and self-conscious in their peaked, felt, hunter-style, cock-feathered caps, wandering about by twos and threes, girl-less, in the town's central square, the Piazza Chanoux, or wandering up and down the via Tillier, the main street, peering wistfully into caffès and restaurants they haven't money enough to go into—much like GIs anywhere.

Curiously, Aosta is still a mining center too, and on a far grander scale than either the Selassi or the Romans could ever have anticipated. There are large iron mines in operation, high in the hills back of the town in what may once have been a tribal stronghold, and one of the big steel companies of Italy, the Acciaieria Cogne, has a plant down the river from the town. The plant and the mines are connected by an aerial cable way, and night and day big ore buckets come down filled and go back empty, between the two.

I drove up there one day to look around. It was easy to see the reason for the cable way—the road is far too steep and treacherous to be practicable for trucking the ore down—and I found a tiny mountain village in a crevice of the hills at the end of it. The mines are not located there, I discovered. They are on the other side of the mountain, at the end of a mile-long tunnel and tramway cut right through the heart of it. It was at first sight a chill and dismal setting. The rock was dark and slaty there; chunks of it mixed with fragments of reddish-brown ore lay strewn about the loading platform at the head of the cable way, and the half-dozen or so houses that formed the village were perched more or less at random on the ledgy slopes around them beneath the dark mouth of the tunnel.

It was late afternoon by the time I got there, and the day was lowering. It had been raining farther down, but here the rain was closer to sleet, and the whole business looked like mining—and living, too—under difficulties.

But the little caffè which served as the town's social center was bright and cheerful, and there were a half-dozen or so men in work clothes seated at the tables who nodded to me gravely, in the friendly but noncommittal mountain fashion, as I came in. It was the padrona, though, who made the place memorable. The level of beauty—or, failing that, of sheer vivacity and charm—is high among Italian women. But there are three or four towns in Italy—the tiny Tiber-side village of Prodi, for one, Gubbio and Orvieto for a couple of others—which shine with a special illumination in my mind because of a particularly beautiful woman I happened to see there.

In Gubbio it was a waitress in a caffè, and in Orvieto it was a clerk sitting wicketed in the main post office; in Prodi, most incongruously, it was a woman, beautifully dressed and extremely soignée, walking across the sun-baked farm-town piazza and smiling discreetly at my open admiration. In the settlement above Aosta (I still don't know the name of the village) it was the proprietress of the caffè.

She was a bit on the short side, full-bodied, broad-faced, brown-skinned, bursting with health, flashing-eyed, warm-mouthed—and no matter how faltering the adjectives I've used to describe her may be she was a real mountain beauty if I ever saw one. No woman who grows up admired can remain totally unaware of her attractiveness. But this one was as nearly unself-conscious as a person could be, and she was also completely content with life in her location.

I ordered a caffè and grappa, and I suppose visitors are rare there, particularly outlanders; when my nationality had been established—"Americano!" she cried in astonishment—I felt, when I couldn't see, the silent scrutiny of the men around and behind me. The padrona, however, was eager to talk. But when I said something about the remoteness of the place—didn't it sometimes seem a little isolated and lonely, even, in the winter?—that, to her, seemed incomprehensible.

"Lonely?" she cried. With the radio? With the television? And they had dances: even in the winter they had dances, and the winters were not bad either. They had snow, of course, and some cold. But they could always get in and out, riding down and back on a car attached to the cable way if necessary. And if there were times when they couldn't— well, what did it matter?

As for Aosta—well, she herself went down every couple of weeks or so to *far la spesa*, or do the marketing. But apart from that, she implied, you could have Aosta, and when she turned to the men for confirmation they all grinned and nodded in silent agreement.

The Alps, too, still figure in the life of Aosta. There is a branch of the Alpine Club of Italy on the Piazza Chanoux, and the square itself, cool and spacious, has a mountain feel about it; it reminded me somehow of the wide main street of Colorado Springs, with Pike's Peak rising beyond it. The year-round ski resort of Courmayeur is only some twenty-odd miles from the town, with a cable-car lift that takes you straight up to the permanent snow fields atop Mont Blanc, and there are several other less well-known resorts in the area.

A good many climbers and skiers use Aosta as their base of operations. Even when we were there, in mid-May, I saw ski boots and climbing boots placed outside the room doors occasionally, for cleaning, at the hotel we stayed at, the Corona è Posta; and one day, coming back to it in the late afternoon, I saw a group of skiers arrive and park their cars in front of it. They were returning, I suppose, from a day's excursion to Courmayeur, and as they straggled in wearily, with the skis slung anyhow over their shoulders, they looked —or I may be pardoned for thinking so—like a band of Praetorians, coming back to camp after a day of forced marching in the mountains.

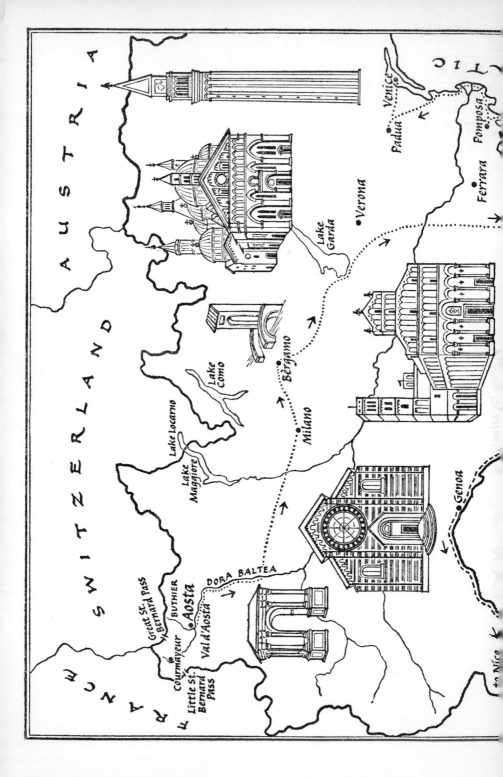

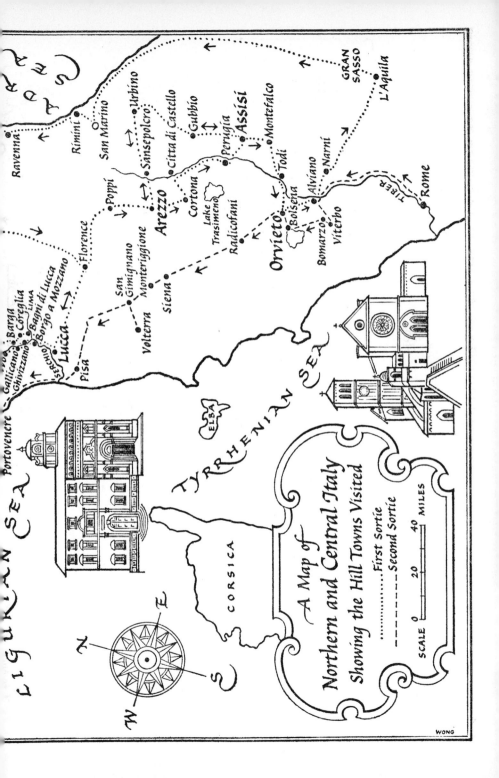

LIGURIAN SEA

ADRIATIC SEA

TYRRHENIAN SEA

Portovenere

Ravenna

Rimini

San Marino

Urbino

Gran Sasso

L'Aquila

Barga
Coreglia
Gallicano
Ghivizzano
Lima
Bagni di Lucca
Borgo a Mozzano
Lucca
Serchio
Pisa

Florence

Poppi

Sansepolcro

Città di Castello

Gubbio

Perugia

Assisi

Montefalco

Narni

Rome

Tiber

San Gimignano
Monteriggione
Volterra
Siena

Arezzo

Cortona

Lake Trasimeno

Radicofani

Orvieto

Todi

Alviano

Bolsena

Bomarzo

Viterbo

ELBA

CORSICA

N
E
W
S

A Map of
Northern and Central Italy
Showing the Hill Towns Visited

.... First Sortie
——————— Second Sortie

SCALE
0   20   40 MILES

WONG

City of Churches

No question about it, France is different from Italy and the Italians are different from the French. Outside the big cities and in the rural areas the people seem poor in both countries, and of the two the Italians seem poorer. There are fewer cars in Italy, or one sees fewer of them on the road than in France, and more motorcycles; more beat-up bicycles than either.

But the Italians appear to mind it less. In France, the motorcyclist or motor-scooter rider goes sternly caparisoned in crash helmet and heavy goggles, while in Italy he is more likely to ride bareheaded; and the cyclists, pedaling manfully up the hills, often have flowers twined around their handle bars. The Italian roads, well paved as they are, are a bit scragglier around the edges, but the houses that line them are brighter in color. In Paris, there are "snack bars" where hot dogs are sold, not to mention such other manifestations as the "strip-tease," a bar called the Crazy Horse Saloon and a night-club revue featuring "Les Sophisticated Ladies." France also has an orange drink called *Vérigoude*.

But outside the tourist centers France is deeply nationalistic; Italy seems less so. Indeed, in recent years there has been a considerable rise in a kind of movie- and television-inspired Americanism, centering chiefly on the legendary West. Young blades in the country towns in Italy wear Levis, properly shrunk and faded, and straw sombreros (also commonly worn by farmers in the fields) and in the Piazza del Commune, the central square in Assisi, I saw one youthful rider of the range actually posting as he rode past behind a friend, on the back seat of a little Lambretta scooter.

The Levis cost considerably more than ordinary Italian work pants. But they are imported from the States and have trade names like "Rifle," "Dogie" and "Roy Rogers," which give them authenticity. They are prominently displayed in the booths at all the town fairs, and I couldn't help feeling that if someone started importing cowboy boots he would make a fortune.

Salt, being a government monopoly, is sold only in cigar stores, and if you have your car washed it is likely to be returned with a sprig of flowers clipped in the door of the glove compartment. France, where the men are always stopping for a *petit coup* of wine or a *café arrosé* with a spot of *eau de vie* or rum, has an alcoholic problem and a severe one.* Italy has none, for there they go in more for wine and even more for frozen sweets like the ice-cream confections called *gelati* and *dolci*. Italy is the only country I know where you'll see grown men going along the streets unabashedly licking ice-cream cones and talking animatedly, and if the nation has no trouble about alcoholism there must be at least some concern about diabetes.

In a sense, perhaps the most significant difference—as our

---

* As attested, when I was last there, by an all-out poster campaign in the Paris Métro and elsewhere, the most plaintive example of which was one headed, *"Papa, ne bois plus, je t'en prie,"* with a picture of a small, pleading boy—reminding me, perversely, of our own American temperance ballad beginning, "Papa, dear Papa, come home with me now. The clock in the steeple strikes ten. . . ."

friend Laurence pointed out—has to do with one of the road signs. Since both countries are invaded annually by motorized tourists of all nations, many of whom have only the most fragmentary knowledge of either language—and couldn't care less—an ingenious system of pictographic signs has been invented for their guidance and information. A big P, for example, means "Parking" (apparently understandable in all tongues). But a P with a red diagonal bar set across it means that parking is prohibited, and the same applies to a picture of a barred automobile horn, at the entrance to towns and villages. (No horn blowing here, in other words, and the rule is strictly enforced.)

Passing on a curve is discouraged in much the same way, except that here the red bar is replaced by a red silhouette of a motorcar, and so on. Well, in both countries the signal that a school lies ahead is a pictograph of two children, school books in hand. But, as Laurence was the first to observe, in France the two children are walking—while in Italy they are running full tilt!

There are deeper differences. France has always been the home of the *arrière pensée*, the cautious approach, and she still is, while in Italy the attitude seems to have grown franker and more open. We ran across an example of this difference as we were crossing the frontier.

This was at the Little St. Bernard Pass, high in the Alps, and the French border guards who examined us there—two short, solidly built men in blue woolen winter uniforms—were the very picture of officialdom. One of them, I remember, the one who appeared to be in charge, carried an enormous clip-board, which he used as a sort of impromptu, portable desk as he checked our license plates, passports, car-registration papers and other such data. His manner was correct but distant, and slightly suspicious; and though he passed us through in the end he seemed at pains to make it clear to us that it was well within his power to stop us right there in our tracks if he wanted to.

Our friend Laurence was driving at the time, and, as I've said, Laurence travels a good deal back and forth between France and Italy. When we came to the Italian border station, a few hundred yards farther on, we were greeted with such enthusiasm by the pair stationed there that I thought that Laurence, having made the trip so often, must surely have gotten to know them.

I was impressed, of course. I am always impressed when I discover that I know somebody who knows somebody else in an official position, even if it's only a policeman. But it turned out that in this case it wasn't so. Laurence actually had never seen either of the men before in his life, and all their cheerful welcomingness, their interest in how we had made the trip up and their concern about the trip down that lay ahead of us—we should have to hurry a little if we were going to get to Aosta before nightfall, I remember they told us—was all just an evidence of their natural ebullience.

I realize, of course, that one mustn't make too much of such isolated incidents. There was deep snow in the passes still and winter in the Alps was barely over; it may be that our French border guard had had a bad lunch or that he just didn't relish his bleak assignment. The Italians, almost frisking about us, obviously liked theirs, for there were skis stacked beside the door of their barrack and ski tracks all over the snow fields rising behind it.

But we ran into much the same attitude of easy, friendly acceptance time after time in Italy, in hotels and restaurants and so on, later on—to the point that occasionally, entering a strange restaurant in a strange town, my wife and I would have the odd, confused feeling that we *must* have been in the place before: everyone seemed so honestly glad to see us—and in the end I couldn't escape the conclusion that the Italians just like *meeting* people, while the French, for some reason, don't.*

There is one respect, however, in which the two countries are joined, or are being joined, and it may do more in the end to wipe out such present differences than any other agency.

This is the network of motor expressways both are building; I was astonished to note how much had been done on them since I had been in Europe last. That had been five years earlier, and at that time there were none in France, while in Italy there were only a few run-down sections left over from the days of Mussolini; there was a certain wry satisfaction for the American to observe what sorry specimens they were—narrow three-lane affairs for the most part, of the sort highway engineers consider death traps, and with any number of equally dangerous grade-level crossings along the way.

Now many of these are being widened and expanded, while a chain of completely modern ones is also in process of building, planned eventually to take the traveler—by way of the Mont Blanc Vehicular Tunnel, also in construction—all the way from Paris to Naples without a break, skirting towns and cities and all other bottlenecks on the way. This, of course, from one point of view, seems a truly breath-taking way of

---

* I add this footnote tentatively. But it has often occurred to me to wonder: can it all be because of the complicated, cumulative aftermath of the War? In the case of the French, it seems to me, it was all so indecisive. In a sense, they still don't know quite what happened to them. They didn't lose the War, precisely, and certainly they didn't win it. Yet in the course of it there was treachery, there were weaknesses revealed and all sorts of other things, and as a result they somehow suddenly found themselves reduced overnight from a first-class power to a position considerably below that: even now, and so long afterward, they are still worrying about it. The Italians, on the other hand, *lost* a war, and so are finished with all that. In matters of such great scale, it occurs to me, it is well to have things clean-cut and decisive.

getting somewhere fast without getting much fun out of it;
but for the European businessman, intent on meeting an
appointment or in getting his trucks through on time, it obviously has its merits.

At any rate, if the new roads, like their American proto-
types, have the advantages of speed and easy, uninterrupted
travel, they have also the same sometimes deadly quality
of uniformity. We left Paris on a short section of this new
European *grand' route*, on our way to Aosta; and on leaving
Aosta later, cut into another longer, larger one, outside of
Milan, being bound by then for the town of Lucca.

I found both pretty much American in pattern, from the
toll booths at the entrances to the curving ramps at the exits,
and including the familiar white- or yellow-striped lanes, the
bounce-back guard rails and the divider strips along the way.
About the only differences, it seemed to me, were that in
France "Esso" and "Shell" signs alternated with "Total" and
"Azur," the native gasolines, and the road is called an "auto-
route"; while in Italy "Shell" and "Esso" alternated with
"Agip," the big Italian trademark, and the word is "autostrada," with an extra syllable for the *u*.

I think, though, it would be a mistake to dismiss all this as
mere imitation. To be sure, the high-speed motor highway
is a peculiarly American phenomenon. More than that, it is
one of our highest accomplishments. Like the pyramid to the
Egyptians, the aqueducts to the Romans, it is one of the
things we do best, and it would be odd indeed if another
people, building for the same purpose, didn't follow our example.

In another sense, though, such roads have a life of their
own, developing their own functions and characteristics according to the demands put upon them. The main demand
is for a minimum of stops. So the services that are necessary
to the care and comfort of the car and its occupants tend
to compact themselves, in Italy as in America: the gas sta-

tion sprouting a restaurant and the restaurant a motel, the motel a novelty shop and so on—and all dedicated to the proposition that it is easier to keep your foot on the gas pedal than it is to shift it to the brake: if you're going to stop for one thing you might as well stop for all.

If in Italy these manifestations have developed a bit differently—the restaurants more innlike and the motels more brightly painted, the shops likely to have their goods on display outside and the whole atmosphere more casual than in America—that only emphasizes the basic similarity of their functions.

We had dinner, one night, in one of the restaurants of the Agip chain, on the outskirts of Aosta, just to see what it was like, and a week or so later had a sort of second breakfast in another, outside Milan. They were about what might be expected by anyone familiar with a Howard Johnson: clean, well lit and efficient; the service competent and quick; and the food, from the pasta to the bistecca and the wine, just a little less good, less individual in flavor, than what we would have had in any trattoria along the old roads or in the towns.

When we stopped at the one outside Milan, I was interested to note that the place, fairly newly opened as it must have been, was already building up a clientele of the same sort of snack-shop barflies—young fellows planted, elbows on the counter, kidding away with the waitress and lingering over a coffee—that one encounters in roadside diners everywhere, but especially in the Midwest. The coffee here was an espresso, instead of the American variety. But the hour was about ten A.M., the place was well outside the limits of Milan and, as has happened to me in America, I couldn't help wondering what brought them there; the waitress wasn't particularly good-looking. At all events—and, again, as in America—they offered a pleasantly leisurely contrast to the rest of the company, gobbling their sandwiches and getting on.

The net result of the autostrada, in any case, is a complete divorcement from the countryside around one, and I got this feeling most strongly in the run across from Milan. There the road traverses the wide, flat plains of the Emilia, and the land is immensely rich and the farming varied. Rice is grown there,* in large, rectangular paddies, only inches deep in water, and when we were there the rice sprouts, sparse in leaf and pale green in color, were just showing above the surface; the men working in them, bare-legged and crouching as they moved along the rows, were mirrored picturesquely in the still waters.

Wine is grown there, too, and it is grown in a peculiarly Italian fashion—each vine planted at the root of a fruit or a nut tree and the tree's branches cut back and trained into the shape of a four- or five-pronged candelabrum; the vines trained up along the branches and then, often, led out in looping festoons from one tree to another. The trees are set out in rows, and the spaces between the rows are planted in grain; and the whole scheme of things, nicely formalized in design as it is, represents a combination of crops and a drain on the soil that would make an American farmer's hair curl.

But the plains of Emilia seem to support it, and there was a kind of country sparkle about the scene—green everywhere, but in varying shades of it, from the darker greens of the trees and the grapevines through the lighter shades of the

* This is a fairly recent development, and I was interested to learn recently, from a friend, that rice is now also grown in the Camargue, the once barren region at the delta of the Rhône, formerly given over, in default of anything else, to the growing of beef cattle. Both, it seems, are concomitants of a growing lack of sure dependence on the rice-growing colonies of both nations in the Orient.

rice to the near-golden tints of the young grain—which made it a pleasure simply to look at.

As is the case elsewhere in Italy, there was little mechanization and the methods were primitive. We saw, a few yards away from the highway, teams of oxen pulling high-wheeled wagons, and donkey carts jogging along the dirt roads between the fields; in the fields themselves, men and women worked with broad-bladed hoes and heavy-helved mattocks that looked as primitive in design as those one sees in the illuminations for a fourteenth-century Book of the Seasons.

We were still not a part of the scene, however. We were cut off from it; and when, as we did farther down and later on in the day we had left Milan, we turned off the autostrada onto a neatly engineered, gently curving exit ramp and, after a short run through an allée of plane trees and a dip through a triple-arched, early-Renaissance gate, found ourselves in the still completely walled city of Lucca, the change was as violent as a drop through four or five centuries.

The city of Lucca itself, in many ways, is a curious mingling of past and present. Maurice Hewlett, a slightly swashbuckling writer of the turn of the century, remarked in his *The Road in Tuscany* on Lucca's "hidden graces" and added, a trifle elliptically, "This may be the reason why nobody goes there. Lucca is one of the least visited towns in Tuscany."

It is still so, by tourists at least; and apart from its bustling, narrow main street, the via Fillungo, and the adjoining piazza, its general atmosphere is quiet, a little reserved, and leisurely. It wasn't always so. Lying more or less halfway between the frequently warring cities of Florence and Pisa, and well within prowling range of the still more powerful Genoa, its past was as turbulent as any, and it was torn by internal warfare besides; everywhere throughout the city, on the towers of churches as well as on those of the palaces, one sees the square-topped battlements that were the marks of the Guelphs confronting the V-shaped ones of the Ghibellines, as the forces within them must have faced each other in earlier times. Ground-floor windows, in Lucca, are still heavily barred, and the street doors staunchly planked—as much, one gathers, to protect against factional strife as to resist invasion.

One gets the feeling, though, that Lucca was drawn into all this bickering somewhat against its will. Dante, who had almost a peasant's shrewdness for sharp characterization, christened it "the city of jobbers" when he visited it in the beginning years of the fourteenth century, and my impression is that whenever it could get loose from its more quarrelsome neighbors for a minute or two Lucca seized the chance gratefully to go in for some honest money-making.

It was famous for its silks and also for its olive oil; and while it was under the rule of Paolo Guinigi, a powerful fifteenth-century merchant prince who was more adept than most at combining business and intrigue, it became, though briefly, one of the foremost banking centers of Italy. Architecturally, its town houses and palaces are, I believe, unique in Italy in that the ground floor was designed to serve as offices and business headquarters, while the family was domiciled in the upper stories—thus neatly compacting home life and business life under one roof.

The most striking of these, incidentally, is the Palazzo Guinigi, on the via Fillungo. Built of brick, with slender marble columns adorning its triple-arched windows, and dating from the fifteenth century, it stands in fairly cramped quarters, to the detriment of its really quite handsome façade. Not so with its tower, however, which rises high above all the surrounding houses and is topped, even more dramatically, by a couple of good-sized ilex trees—come there no one actually knows how, but most probably from seeds carried in the droppings of birds, and deposited generations ago.

Though it has long since lost any pretense to importance as a business center, Lucca is still prosperous. There is a big tobacco-processing plant outside the town and its olive-oil production is still considerable; if one doesn't see many tourists one does see a good many Italian businessmen in well-cut silk suits and carrying brief cases, hurrying across the Piazza Napoleone, the largest of the central squares. (The Piazza gets its name, incidentally, because Napoleon, after his conquest of Italy, rewarded Lucca's loyalty to him by giving the town, entire, to his sister, who bore the charming name of Elisa Baciocchi, or "kiss eyes." Her residence was in the huge and rather rambling Palazzo Ducale, whose imposing façade occupies one side of the square. She held it scarcely more than a decade, however; in 1815, after Napoleon's empire itself collapsed, it fell to the Dukes of Parma, and from their hands it went to Tuscany a couple of decades later. Things moved fast in those lively days.)

To me, though, Lucca is unique for a different reason; like the Borough of Brooklyn, Lucca is the City of Churches. I had neither the means nor the inclination to count them all, but I was told that there are at least twenty-five in the town, and since Lucca is an extraordinarily compact little place that amounts to a sizable number.

Churches, literally, are everywhere. There are small ones, like Sant'Anastasio, with its prim, red-and-white banded, brick and marble façade, or the really ancient Santa Maria Nera, dedicated to the legendary "Black Mary," the handmaiden of the Virgin on her wanderings. These lie hidden up narrow side streets or stand wedged into widenings at the ends of alleys. And there are the big ones, like San Michele with its soaring façade, the Cattedrale of San Martino or the more venerable, burly-looking San Frediano, which stand isolated on squares or piazze of their own.

Their bells, banging, bonging, clanging in mutually interrupting, intermingling rhythms, were the first things I heard in the morning and the last at night; and when I walked around the town by day, as they struck the hours and the quarters, I would find the tones of the chorus changing subtly as I moved from one circle of sound to another. It may be no accident that two major composers, Luigi Boccherini, the eighteenth-century master of chamber music, and the operatic composer, Giacomo Puccini, were born and grew up here, in sound of the bells. (So, too, however, was Castruccio Castracani, one of the most ruthless of the thirteenth-century condottieri.)

All the churches are Romanesque in style. They are fairly closely grouped chronologically too. The oldest is Santa Maria Nera, which dates from around the year 1000. But the majority were completed in the thirteenth and fourteenth centuries, at the height of the Romanesque, and I was, I must confess, unprepared for it.

To one, who was "brought up," so to speak, as I was, on French Gothic, the Romanesque always seemed a singularly ungraceful and awkward style. Until I came to Lucca—and it was a lucky thing for me that I did—I found it hard to accustom myself to it.

Since the Romanesque builders never learned, or never quite understood, the liberating influence of the flying buttress—each arching, bow-taut buttress acting, in a sense, as an airy underpinning for the upper walls, letting them rise higher and higher—there is at first something heavy and forbidding about their structures. Nothing soars in Romanesque; the very weight of the walls prevents such aspirations, and when height is really attempted, as in the largest churches, the massing of masonry necessary to attain it leaves one with the impression that he is confronted by an engineering feat rather than an architectural accomplishment: one feels *under* it, rather than *in* it.

The basic design—a high, raftered nave, flanked at times by low, pent-roofed side aisles, all running down to a small,

semicircular apse and vestigial transepts—has a curiously barn-
like appearance; while such outer decoration as is customarily
added—the false galleries tiered across the façade, and so on
—seems always a mere embellishment, as of course it is, instead of deriving from any structural necessity. The interior,
since it lacks a clerestory—that wonderful row of high windows, slanting light down into the Gothic cathedrals—is
usually dim and a little somber: again, forbidding, instead of
being truly welcoming.

So much for the faults in the Romanesque style. Yet for all
that I was interested to see how many variations the Luccan
builders were able to play on so fundamentally simple a design, and in the end I wound up pretty much converted to
it—though I find it difficult now to describe the processes of
my conversion. It seems to me, however, that its very simplicity is a factor.

You could design a Romanesque church with no more than
a compass and a T square. But you could do the same thing
with a Purist painting, and in both cases it is the harmony of
the arrangement that counts. Inside the church, it's the march
of the columns down the nave and their relation to the size
and weight of the structure. In the exterior, the three plain
barrel-arched portals of the façade and the windows and galleries above must be spaced just right or the whole effect—
depending as it does on the sheer geometry of the design—
will fail. Underneath its apparent rusticity, Romanesque is a
strictly ordered style. But then, so is that of a good Pennsyl-
vania barn.*

* Later on, one day in the Upper Church of San Francesco at Assisi, I
was stopped dead in my tracks by a sudden vista I had through a portal,
halfway down one of the side aisles. Through the opening one could
see a section of another portal, and through that a section of stone
stairway, unrailed, ascending diagonally. All was straight lines and
rectangles. All was the same pale, heavenly pink of the Assisi stone—
and all, too, was as serenely *right* in its proportions as the most perfect
Purist composition.

But a church is harder to describe than a painting or a piece of sculpture. All sorts of things enter in, both structural and utilitarian, while even the site and the surroundings have their value. I can't help wondering, for instance, if Santa Maria Nera would have looked so striking to me if I hadn't stumbled on it unexpectedly one evening when the vertical stone spandrels, elegantly slim and beautifully spaced, which form its main—indeed, almost its only—outer decoration, were put into bold relief by the moonlight; or if I should have liked the placid little church of San Giustino, as small and unpretentious as a country cottage, quite so much if there hadn't been a solid row of roosting pigeons, chuckling and cooing companionably, all along the eaves as I passed there by day.

At all events, the churches of Lucca vary widely in their emotional evocation, in the atmosphere they suggest. The single round window of San Francesco, with its smaller, petal-like fringe of smaller ovate apertures, together with the single, plain portal below, gives a charming quality of prim decorousness to the face; while the slightly larger church of San Giusto, still plain in general design and with its stone face looking more than usually weathered, but with a pair of sculptured lions (those recurrent symbols of the Romanesque) staring down from above the main portal, has an air of worn but still venerable dignity.

Among the larger ones, San Frediano—big enough to have a piazza of its own and a campanile that rises higher than any other in town—wears a broad-shouldered, swaggering look that goes well indeed with the concept one forms of its namesake: St. Frigidian, as he is known in the Anglo-Saxon terminology. Born an Ulsterman around the first quarter of the sixth century, he was one of those now legendary walking-preaching monks who came out of Ireland when it was almost the sole repository of culture in the Dark Ages, to spread the Gospel over Europe.

In his case, his way led him into Italy, where he lived as a hermit for some years on the slopes of Monte Pisano, in the massif east of Pisa; performed several miracles—including, according to legend, the diversion of the course of the Serchio River, which till then, flowing through Lucca, had periodically flooded it—and ended his mortal days as Bishop of Lucca.*

San Martino, the Duomo or Cathedral of the galaxy, is another one of those which profit by their location, for the piazza before it, though smaller than the Piazza Napoleone, is nevertheless the center of a good deal of the town's activities. Interurban buses arrive and depart from it, noisily, and the square is lined with small stands selling cakes, sandwiches and the inevitable gelati or ice-cream confections, to help tide people over the rigors of their journey—on all of which the church, with its unusually deep, triple-arched porch and three-galleried, calm façade, looks down benignly.

It is apparently a loved church, too—or was it my unfamiliarity at the time with the Italians' passion for scratching or scribbling their names, initials or other memorabilia of their passage on every available wall surface that made me think so? At any rate, the inner walls of the porch of San Martino are covered with such graffiti, and I was able to prove, over and over again, a favorite theory of mine, that there's no need to carve your initials on tree trunks or inscribe them on the pillars of subway platforms. Someone has always already been there to do it for you; and at San Martino I discovered several R.C.'s—one dated as far back as 1893, which gave it a certain flavor of antiquity—already inscribed in advance commemoration of my presence.†

* It was Leonardo, wasn't it, who, when in the service of Florence, and by engineering skill rather than divine intervention, diverted the course of the Arno, and made Pisa an inland city, instead of a seaport? But again this is something I heard in passing, and it may be legend, too.
† This passion for immortalizing themselves, or at least their initials, goes so far among the Italians that many of the churches have placards

Loveliest of all of the big churches, though, is San Michele. Faced with a white Carrara marble that has been toned by the centuries to a mixture of cream and ivory, laced with loggias and intricately columned, it is a confection by day and—floodlit as it is—by night a true apparition of beauty.

It is a church that, perhaps because Lucca itself is little visited, is seldom cited by the experts. But to me it represents something close to perfection in the Romanesque, and if some of its charm derives from its surroundings, and some is the result of a happy accident, that hardly alters the total effect.

Its site is particularly fortunate; for, in contrast to the cramped location of some of the Luccan churches, the piazza it sits on—once, indeed, the Roman forum: the church's full name is San Michele in Foro—is particularly wide and spacious, and the houses around it, including the old, arcaded mercato set catercorner from it, are all-of-a-piece architecturally. The campanile, with four tiers of fretted windows relieving and punctuating its height—offsetting, too, any suggestion of grimness, for in many of the churches the bell tower is also, all too obviously, a tower planned for defense—for once does not dwarf the church, as so many others do. It has no battlements, either, atop.

The accident—the happy accident—lies in the fact that originally, and apparently in the midst of construction, plans

---

on the walls, some stern and minatory, some almost plaintive, forbidding the practice. They have small effect, and I was interested to note that the degree of sanctity of the surroundings acts not as a deterrent but rather as an incitement. In the small, dimly lighted crypt of Santa Chiara, at Assisi, where the supposedly incorruptible body of the saint is laid out in her nun's costume in a glass-walled tomb and the atmosphere fairly breathes of reverence, I was surprised to see the marble walls roundabout covered with what at first I took to be cobwebs—until, looking closer, I perceived that it was really a network of tiny, neatly inscribed, often fairly ancient initials. Though I'm not particularly religious myself, I confess to being a bit horrified at that, as at a sacrilege.

were altered to include a considerably higher nave than had first been contemplated, and the façade was heightened proportionately. Funds ran out, though, as they seem to have had a habit of doing with Italian churches; the new nave was never built, and as a result the flat façade towers almost steeple-high over the body of the church.

It occurs to me now, as I write, that I may be alone in my fondness for Lucca's San Michele, and I feel myself feeling like hedging a little. It is true, then, that the church, in a conventional sense, is badly proportioned. The frontal face *is* slablike in its inordinate elevation; there are times indeed when, looking at it, one is reminded of those false-fronted houses—pretending to be two stories high from the street side, when there was only one story behind—that one used to see in the mining camps in the West.

But on the other hand, the rearing façade is, for once, a proper match for the campanile, which gives a certain sense of unity to the whole design. And what a wealth, what an almost Oriental profusion of inventiveness there is in the exterior ornamentation, most particularly in the treatment of the fluted, voluted, utterly purposeless but also completely charming, close-ranked columns supporting the loggie topping both the façade and the sides. It's a church that I found myself coming back to with pleasure, again and again.

If I've gone on so long about Lucca's churches, it is because that is where—for me, at least—the greater part of the town's interest centers. There is a famous baptismal font near the entrance, inside San Frediano. Dating from the twelfth century, huge, heavy and bulbous, studded with rough-carved heads of monstrous, mythical figures, it has an almost barbaric magnificence that attracted us. And in San Martino, alone in one of the transepts, is perhaps the greatest of Lucca's "hidden graces," and one of the real masterpieces of sculpture of the fifteenth century in Italy.

This is the sarcophagus of Ilaria, the young wife of the

Paolo Guinigi I've already mentioned, by Jacopo della Quercia. It is a remarkable piece for many reasons, chief among them being the fact that, for once in funerary sculpture, all sense of the tragic or awesome has been avoided.

Instead, Della Quercia, a Sienese, concentrated on the youth and freshness of his subject, and the lady lies there, full length, a pillow under her head and, at her feet, a small, nuzzling dog—in those days, a symbol of fidelity. Her hands are lightly folded; and she is clothed in a robe whose long, straight folds accentuate the slenderness of the body—the whole pose, almost magically, suggesting sleep, a little catnap really, rather than death.

There are the ramparts. Built of brick and imposingly high, revetted and dry-moated in the best Flemish fashion, these were completed in the sixteenth century, and there is a certain mild irony in the fact that they were erected at a time when Lucca's warfaring days were just about over. Like some of our modern battleships, Lucca's walls are ending their days without ever having been fired upon, and as a result they stand intact, ringing the city in a rough circle some three to four miles around.

Their broad, continuous top has long ago been parked and planted in plane trees, these now grown impressively high. (Lucca, incidentally, is as proud of its plane trees as Florence is of its cypresses or Rome of its pines.) I can think of few pleasanter things than a walk along the ramparts beneath them—the town with its churches and towers lying as if diked on the one side, and on the other the olive- and vine-planted fields rolling off towards the grayish-blue, wavering line of the Apennines, on the horizon.

At such moments the autostrada, roaring along in the middle distance, seems centuries away indeed.

Pilgrims to Piero

Maurice Hewlett, whom I have quoted appreciatively before, speaks in his *The Road in Tuscany* of Arezzo as "a prosperous country town in a fold of the hills." The tone is a little slighting and the image the phrase calls up is of peace and rusticity, and after a visit to the place it seems to me that in both respects Mr. Hewlett could hardly have been wronger. Its atmosphere is far from peaceful, in my experience, and instead of being a farming village Arezzo is essentially a hill town—but one that seems to have slid down the side of its hill, landing, in a sense, in the lap of a busy *borgo*, or suburb, in the level areas below.

The result is to give a curiously tilted arrangement to everything: in Arezzo—as for that matter also in its neighbor, Siena—even the central piazza slants. The true hill town—a phenomenon more or less peculiar to the two central provinces of Umbria and Tuscany, straddling the Apennines north of Rome—is an eyrie, a crow's nest for humans. Walled for defense, and protected if possible by a series of cliffs as well, with its houses huddled around a church, a square and a castle, it sits on top of its own craggy little hill, remote and self-contained, more or less impregnable except by siege—standing now, for all the charm of its tortuous, cobblestoned alleys and crumbling battlements, as a monument to the violence of the days which gave it its form.

Arezzo still preserves some vestiges of this framework. It has its castle, or the ruins of one, on the crest of the hill; and a huge one it was, for it was a stronghold of the fourteenth-century fighting bishop, Guido Tarlati, and later of the Medicis, under Cosimo I, whose blazon is still over the heavy, portcullised portal, and there are sections of the old walls, built by Tarlati, to be seen roundabout. (Incidentally, I came across a fresco by Benozzo Gozzoli in the church of San Francesco, in the small town of Montefalco, on the Umbrian side of the mountains, showing Arezzo in its old, completely walled state; and it looked as tight and compact as any other hill town. So much for Hewlett, and his "country" village.)

Arezzo's history goes back far beyond all this, however, to the extent that its actual origins are unknown. Even in Etruscan times, its importance was considerable, for it was one of a league of twelve towns that was formed to resist the Roman expansion, and when the Romans took over it was able to make peace with them on more or less equal terms.

The Aretines, traditionally, are supposed to be shrewd, witty and irreverent (a set of qualities that were combined in the person of one Pietro Aretino, a sixteenth-century gossip writer who is supposed to have invented the lampoon and was, in effect, the Walter Winchell of his day) but they seem to have had a habit of guessing wrong politically. Arezzo sided with Marius in the Civil Wars, and was reduced to slave status by Sulla, his conqueror, in consequence; and again, a century or so later it picked Pompey against Caesar, and was severely punished again. In the Middle Ages and the Renaissance, it was constantly embroiled, and usually to its disadvantage, with such neighboring towns as Siena, Florence and Cortona; and as late as the close of the eighteenth century it even staged a brief revolt against the French occupation, and was sacked a year later in consequence.

Politics aside, it is still—or I found it so—a nervous town, bustling and noisy. Formerly, it had a leaning for the arts. In Etruscan times, it was famous for its pottery and ceramics, and later on it was the home of Petrarch, Guido d'Arezzo (the monkish musicologist who invented the musical scale) and that Boswell of Renaissance artists, Giorgio Vasari.

After a fairly brief visit there, of some four or five days, I began to feel that a share of that nervy, nervous energy is a bit misdirected. Arezzo is a late town, even for Italy. Well after midnight, in the lower part of the town particularly, the bars are still crowded; groups of youngsters wearing Levis, jumpers and beards—the Italian version of the hep-cat—stand as close as they can to juke boxes playing American hot-jazz records turned up as loud as the machine can stand, and afterward can be heard trooping, catcalling and singing through the streets. Arezzo is the only town in Italy I saw where youthful exuberance seems tinged with a trace of delinquency; there were times at night when I felt the same uneasiness that one might on a side street in New York, going past a group of youths standing under an arc light on a corner.

In the field of history and art, I discovered a good many things worth noting in Arezzo. The fourteenth-century Duomo, the town cathedral, standing facing the fortress across a pleasant little park at the crest of the hill, is a bit on the heavy side. It is one of those churches of a type I spoke of in an earlier chapter: one feels *under* it rather than *in* it, and the exterior has been much "restored." It contains, however, the tomb of the truculent Bishop Tarlati, a somberly imposing marble affair in the form of a sarcophagus, with a series of panels in bas-relief along the side, grimly cataloguing his triumphs, from his consecration as a bishop through the various sieges and battles he engaged in (Lucignano, Chiusi, Focognano, Rondine and so on: the Bishop, as head of the

Ghibelline party, was the terror of the small towns of Tuscany); a series of sparkling Della Robbia reliefs in gleaming ceramic; and a curiously haughty-looking Mary Magdalene, not to my mind one of his best works, by Piero della Francesca.

I found the smaller parish church, of Santa Maria della Pieve, a little way farther down the hill on the via Dei Pileati, much more to my liking. Dating mostly from the eleventh and twelfth centuries, it has a beautifully balanced façade, made up of three tiers of gracefully colonnaded galleries or loggias rising airily over the portals, and a campanile that is pierced on all sides by arched fenestrations to give a feeling of lightness unusual in such early works.

Behind it, in the old Piazza Grande, is a perfect little jewel of a house called the Palazzo della Misericordia, named after a lay organization of the Renaissance called La Confraternità della Misericordia, devoted to charity and good works. I shan't try to describe it in too great detail. The greater part of it, I suppose, must be classed as Renaissance, for it was completed in the sixteenth century. But the portal, constructed a century or so earlier, is done in a kind of miniature Gothic; there's a lacy little loggia set in under the eaves, with an innocently Baroque small bell tower above, and the whole represents a happy juncture of styles that in its capriciousness reminded me somehow of some of the equally whimsically confected palazzi of Venice.

Apart from the immortal Misericordia, the Piazza itself is more consistent, architecturally. Irregular in shape and like most of Arezzo sloping irregularly too, lined with old houses, many of them with deep wooden balconies and broad-eaved roofs in the Tuscan fashion, it has a wonderful kind of museum quietness and completeness about it—or it has when the lads of Arezzo, irreverent as ever, aren't using its gradient as a testing ground for their motor scooters. Every afternoon at around five o'clock, while I was there, they congregated in front of a couple of small caffès at the lower corner, licking ice-cream cones and gunning their motors while still in the saddle, and then, on unpredictable impulse, roaring off for a tour of the square and a return for more gelati.

The great glory of the town, however, and the main thing that brings visitors to it now, is a series of frescoes called "The Story of the True Cross" by Piero della Francesca, filling the choir of the church of San Francesco, a big, gaunt, thirteenth-century edifice on the via Cavour, halfway down the hill from the Piazza Grande. It was not always such a Mecca for art lovers, and Piero's reputation rose and fell in the course of past centuries; it is only lately that it has risen again, higher than ever.

Born early in the fifteenth century in the tiny neighboring town of Borgo Sansepolcro, where he also seemed to have lived the major part of his life, Piero (as he's now familiarly known) appears to have had a fair amount of success in his lifetime.* But it was more with his fellow artists than with

---

* In view of his ups and downs, I can't help commenting on the irony of the fact that Piero della Francesca, so long ignored, is now included in the select group of artists who, like royalty, are known only by their first names or, in some instances, by their nicknames. Titian is one. His full name, of course, was Tiziano Vecellio. Giotto is another. His family name was di Bondone, and Giotto is a diminutive of Angelo, or Angelotto. Masaccio merely means "Fat Tom," short for Tommaso di Ser Giovanni di Mone, while Perugino and Veronese are simply place names, meaning Pietro Vannucci from Perugia and Paolo Cagliari from Verona, respectively. There must be other Leonardos as there are at least a couple of other Pieros—di Cosimo and Polliauolo—but these are all in the slightly lower, or full-name, category; yet among those in the know to say "Piero della Francesca" (also, in a sense, another nickname: it means "Peter of the French mother") has become a kind of intellectual redundancy. To the initiate "Piero" alone suffices.

All this, it occurs to me, is in exact opposition to the current tendency, where the *last* name—Picasso, Leger, Buffet, Rouault and so on— is the sign of top status. If Michelangelo were alive today, he would probably sign himself "Buonarroti," and Raphael, "Di Sanzio." On reflection, I think I like the old way better. It seems cozier.

the general public or the important patrons, and even by the artists he was respected as much as a theorist and mathematician as he was as a painter. (One of the early serious students of the then new science of perspective, he wrote a couple of treatises on the subject which were highly regarded, as indeed they still are: his approach to the geometry of objects in space was apparently mathematically so sound that—a fact I ran across only recently—his works are still valued by experts in airplane design.)

Later on, his painting style, sharply linear, cool, clear and precise, seemed so completely at variance with the more opulent Italianate manner then preferred that he fell into almost total eclipse in the couple of centuries that followed. As late as the nineteenth century, the approach of the critics was cautious. Though Berenson—and the fact is greatly to his credit—was one of the first to recognize Piero as a real master, he was always a trifle uncertain in his approach to the man. What troubled him, again, was the lack of overt emotionality; and as time went on he seems almost to have regretted his own early enthusiasm, finding Piero "opposed to the manifestation of feeling," complaining that his portrait heads were "conceived as if they were objects in nature, rocks, hills . . . landscapes," and referring to the figure of Christ in his "Resurrection" at Sansepolcro as "that sturdy stevedore." (It was merely a "manly specimen," in an earlier version.) About the best thing Berenson could do for him, in the end, was to compare him with Cézanne; but this, again, was faint praise, for Berenson, always uncomfortable in the presence of modern painting (he could never get over a suspicion that Picasso was an imposter) didn't much care for Cézanne.

The comparison with Cézanne is astute, however, though it rests more on the two men's lives and attitudes than on any resemblance in their art. Both were shy, dogged, rustic, painstaking and slow-working. (The Sansepolcro chapter of the Confraternità della Misericordia, no doubt familiar with their fellow townsman's rate of production, allotted him three years to complete an altarpiece it commissioned from him in 1442, and the work apparently dragged on long beyond that, since it wasn't paid for until 1462.)

Otherwise, not a great deal is known about Piero. The exact year of his birth has not been established, though it seems agreed that it must have been between 1410 and 1420; the first definite date that can be assigned to him is 1439 when, aged either nineteen, twenty-nine or somewhere between (the last being the most likely) he was working in the studios of Domenico Veneziano, in Florence, who may be taken as his principal teacher. The rest of his life, seen through a tissue of chance references in contemporary church records, court chronicles and other documents, and including a certain amount of sheer guesswork, is even more shadowy than those of most others in that vanished era.

He was in Rome in 1459, working on some frescoes in the Vatican which, along with a lot of his other works, have now vanished; and a few years later he was at the court of that famous contemporary patron of the arts, Federico da Montefeltro, Duke of Urbino, where he painted two of those portraits, of the Duke and his wife, Battista Sforza, which Berenson found so stony—as well as a "Flagellation" scene, the interpretation of which has been a cause of controversy ever since. Piero, for all his strict, naturalistic approach, had an almost surrealist, mystical side, too: a great many of his paintings have suggestions of double, and even triple, meanings.

He was at Rimini too, for a while, and also at Ferrara, painting something (again, vanished) for the powerful D'Estes. But none of these towns is very far from his native Sansepolcro, and between times he seems to have come homing back there, where his local eminence was such that he served for a time as Town Councillor. He was also, according to the town records, once fined for non-payment of taxes, which argues either an artist's absent-mindedness or an equally Bohemian lack of funds. He died there—having gone totally blind in his last years, according to Vasari, though this again is disputed—in 1492.

The picture one gets from all this is of a partial recluse, a man happiest with the simplicities of small-town existence, whose very retiringness left him ill-fitted for the highly competitive, fashionable life of a court like that at Urbino (it was there and at about the same time that Baldassare Castiglione wrote his *Book of the Courtier*, discussing and dissecting the social graces, with especial emphasis on the arts of love) and there seems no doubt that his lack of ambition, as much as the astringent quality of his art, helped deprive him of any great amount of popular success. It's true too that he could go wrong occasionally, carrying monumentality to the point of impassivity.

Yet it is hard for the modern eye to see how anyone could look at the Arezzo frescoes, "The Story of the True Cross," without respect and wonder. There are plenty of other instances in Renaissance Italy where one artist was commissioned, lavishly, to fill a whole room or chapel with pictures, from the Giottos at Assisi to the Carpaccios at Venice and the Signorellis at Orvieto, and the magnificence of the idea is always breath-taking. In almost every case I know of, however, they tell their stories, so to speak, seriatim, incident by incident; it was Piero alone who—and it seems to me his greatest triumph—had the breadth of vision and the imaginative capacity to develop his as a unified conception, fusing it into a whole, and so making the three sides of the choir at Arezzo into what amounts to a single picture.

The story itself is a mixture of pageantry, fantasy and, to be frank about it, pure nonsense. Essentially, it's the account of the growth of a tree whose wood, by the fact that it was used in the making of the Cross, was destined to be hallowed, and it begins with the planting of its seed, symbolically, in the mouth of the dying Adam. After that, there are dreams, inter-

positions of the Queen of Sheba, King Solomon, the Emperor
Constantine and other figures, all revolving around the career
of the tree and including the Jews, who, led by a totally ana-
chronistic Judas, emerge as the villains of the piece, first using
its timbers to construct the Cross, then hiding it and at last
being forced to disclose it. (In medieval times, by a convolu-
tion of thought almost impossible to follow now, it was forgotten that Christ himself was a Jew; it is always they, in the
legendry of the epoch, who persecute Him, and not the Romans.) The story ends with a miracle, in which the holy
properties of the Cross are disclosed, and its subsequent return, in pomp, to Jerusalem.

Piero has handled all this rather cavalierly, abandoning
consecutiveness in favor of a more integrated plastic development. There are fourteen panels in all, disposed in three tiers,
and the artist has arranged them so that their compositional
progression is naturally upward, with the two big battle
scenes occupying the lowest sections, the less crowded incidents generally just above, and the airiest, quietest ones at the
top—like the death of Adam, which occurs in open countryside. The colors follow this progression, grading up from
darker tones to lighter, cooler ones as the eye moves upward,
and the result is to give a kind of natural, organic unity to the
composition, as of a movement from earth to sky.

Because of the neglect into which Piero and his paintings
fell, some sections of the frescoes are in bad condition. On
the other hand, for the same reason, they have suffered little
from retouching or "restoration"; and so the original color
pattern, though faded, is still intact, and here the impression
is of pale, almost silvery tones, the greens, blues and yellows
predominating.

For all the overall unity of the conception, there are separate panels that stand out and, within the panels, separate
details—the "Dream of Constantine," for example, a truly
hauntingly beautiful, dimly lighted night scene, in which the

Emperor is shown lying tented on the field on the eve of battle, dreaming of the Cross which was to carry him to victory over Maxentius next morning; the gracefully composed "Arrival of the Queen of Sheba at the Court of Solomon," where the Queen and her retinue are seen before the palace, against a background of green, hilly countryside (it was she, according to the story, who prophesied that the wood of the Cross would have mystical powers, and so set off the search for it); and, among the small, remarkable details, the friezelike array of devout, intently watching spectators, gathered prayerfully to observe the miracle by which the Cross, lowered over the body of a dead youth, reveals itself to be the true one by reviving him.

All art, or our appreciation of it, is ambiguous, the very qualities that appeal to one generation often being the ones that repel another. Lionello Venturi, one of the closest students of Piero's work, says somewhere that "it is always high noon" in his paintings and this, it seems to me, has the kind of ambivalence that I'm speaking of. It is intended as praise now, and it is aptly phrased to describe the cool, sourceless illumination and the sense of timelessness of his work. (It's worth noting, I think, that none of Piero's figures, clearly outlined but lightly modeled within the outlines, ever casts a shadow.) But it could still, by a mere change of emphasis— the coolness turning to chill and the clarity to severity—have been used in dispraise rather less than a century ago.

Because of this constant shifting of values, it's important too, in my view, for the critic to avoid any sense of smugness in dealing with the opinions of previous periods. There were few, after all, who appreciated Cézanne in his lifetime.

Even so, I find it difficult to understand those who for so long a time dismissed Piero as "lacking in feeling." We went out one day, while in Arezzo, to Sansepolcro—a painless pilgrimage, certainly, since the town is only about forty miles away and the trip throughout is through lovely, lush, rolling Tuscan farmland. (Michelangelo, incidentally, was born in Caprese, only ten or twelve miles farther north.)

Sansepolcro, small, partially walled, is still pretty much a village—so rustic, indeed, that they have to have signs barring ox carts from the center of it—and apart from the main street and a large, dusty piazza the town is a labyrinth of narrow, cobbled streets and winding, lanelike alleys. Giulia Buitoni, matriarch of the prosperous American Buitoni ravioli- and spaghetti-making clan, was born there as well as Piero, though of course considerably later; and honors now are about equally divided. There's a well equipped public athletic field called the Campo Sportivo Buitoni just outside the gates—an addition to the town's recreational facilities which I'm sure Town Councillor della Francesca would have approved of—and in a small, grassy square not far from the central piazza a statue of the Councillor himself.

It shows him standing, hawk-nosed, heavy-browed and rather arrogant in bearing, his palette in one hand and a brush in the other, and dressed, elegantly if perhaps a shade incongruously, in a flowing, richly furred cape and furred Florentine cap, and with, at his feet, a stack of books and manuscripts to symbolize his theoretical writings. The whole effect is a bit grandiose, as of an artist at work on what he knows is a set piece, and I've a feeling that the unassuming Piero might have been a bit taken aback by this heavy-handed impression of him.

My main objective at Sansepolcro was Piero's painting of the "Resurrection"—that manly specimen or husky stevedore according as one looks at it—in Sansepolcro's Palazzo Communale or Town Hall; I found it well worth the trip to see it. As I've said, I still boggle at the accusation that Piero's work is lacking in feeling. Certainly, there are no passionate extremes, no grandiloquent effects to be found there; what one gets instead is a kind of gentle poignance—a feeling, if I may

put it so, that one is in the presence of a man of infinite understanding—and the more effective for the fact that the feeling
is restrained.

The design of the "Resurrection" is almost mathematically
symmetrical. Christ is shown full-face and full-figured, dead-
centered in the picture and half-arisen from the coffin,
crowned, robed, still bleeding from the wound in his chest
and holding a banner emblazoned with a cross as if it were a
battle flag. Four sleeping soldiers lie sprawled before the
coffin in front of him, and Berenson was right, at least, in
accenting the virility of the Christ figure: though the face is
grave and the eyes almost accusing, the overall effect is one of
immense confidence, strength and assurance.

He seems less to have arisen than to have sprung there, and
He seems ready too with one more leap to go further, upward
and outward. This feeling of immense, almost overflowing
vitality is increased by the tonal treatment, and this is done
without the slightest resort to melodramatics. No shafts of
light streak down to signal the Resurrection, and there are no
sepulchral shadows surrounding the sleeping soldiers.

All are in that light of high noon that Venturi speaks of;
but, as Laurence pointed out while we were studying the
painting, by the subtlest possible gradations of color it is the
Christ, pink, warm-fleshed, who seems most alive, while
the live but sleeping soldiers, greenish-faced, livid, lie as if
death had overtaken them. To convey so profound a meta-
physical concept so subtly and yet so simply seems to me an
accomplishment of the highest order.

A Trip Up the Serchio

One of the things I had planned to do in the course of this trip to Italy was to spend some time in the lesser-known towns in the hills of Umbria and Tuscany, but it wasn't until we were staying in Lucca that I made my first excursion among them. These are the towns—the villages, really—that have little or nothing to recommend them in the way of architecture or art. They have no history either, or not much that is easily discoverable. All they have is their antiquity, and since antiquity lies all around you in Italy—antiquity, too, of an almost unmeasurable sort, frequently going back far beyond even Etruscan times—they go generally unmentioned in the guidebooks and are little visited. But they represent, in a sense, the hill town *per se*, unchanged more or less from its beginnings; and this and their rusticity give them a kind of innocent charm that the better-known places lack.

Perugia, after all, is still called a hill town, as indeed it is. But the old town, sitting superbly on top of its hill, has been all but swamped by the rising tide of woolen mills, cement plants and iron foundries, not to mention the big Perugina candy factory that has grown up the slopes below it. San

How steep these hill towns are! This is Assisi, slanting uphill from our hotel terrace.

(Right) Aosta—*proof, if proof were needed, that the Romans, two thousand years or so ago, were here.*

And this is Orvieto, seen sidewise, and steeper still.

Lucca—piazza and church of San Francesco

Cloisters are always cool, calm and quiet. This one is in Aosta, at the twelfth-century church of Sant' Orso.

Lucca—the frosting-white church of San Michele, with a good view of the famous false front.

Ghivizzano—the keep

(Right) A side alley—almost anywhere, but probably in the Garfagnano. But how sunny, how peaceful, and how clean!

The corduroy-patterned roofs of Ghivizzano

Castelnuovo di Garfagnana—the moat-path under the fortifications.

Market day in one of the towns of the Garfagnano. They are always fun.

Gimignano has suffered less (or prospered less, depending on how you look at it) from industrialization, and so has Assisi. But both have become so widely known for their artistic treasures that with the growth of organized tourist travel they have practically been turned into bus stops.

Every day, throughout the tourist season, the big sight-seeing buses that the Italians call "Pullmans" come pounding up the winding approach roads; disgorge their small self-conscious bands of trippers, all in a clump in the central piazza, for the brisk guided tour through the Museo Civico, the churches and the other highlights; and then, loaded again and all noses counted, go pounding off, this time with much popping of exhausts and horn-hooting at the curves, on their way to the next item on the itinerary.

San Marino, though its perch on the very pinnacle of an inverted V of solid rock makes it almost the quintessence of the hill town (I shall never forget my first sight of it, at night across a plain, its lights dangling in a converging cluster, improbably high in the sky) has been turned, by day, by the sheer, indomitable industry of its citizenry, into a sort of Coney Island of souvenir shops, English-, German- and French-spoken restaurants and strenuously scrubbed, landscaped and "restored" fortifications. We were especially abashed to discover this, for we'd gone out of our way—away out of our way, in fact—to get to the Republic of San Marino, under the impression that it was probably very little visited. Like the people who "leave early" after a week end in the country, we found that a lot of others had had the same notion.

Most such places are what they are largely because their inhabitants, five or six centuries ago, had the acumen, or the luck, to engage some later-to-be-famous artists to do the decorations for their churches and palaces, and had had the strength or tenacity to hold onto them. What I was interested in was the humbler type of hill town, and luckily for me the supply in Italy is practically inexhaustible, for as time went on and I saw more of them I grew more and more fascinated by them.

Every hill, it sometimes seems—and Italy, with the spine of the Apennines running down its length, is an extremely rugged and mountainous country—has its beckoning, battlemented keep and its tight little huddle of houses around it, the whole surrounded by a drift of crumbling walls down along the slope; and though the basic structure of one is as like to another as the façades of the inevitable small, weathered stone- or brick-fronted Romanesque churches always fronting on the main piazza, there are enough variations on that simple design to make them, to me at least, endlessly intriguing. In a sense, the towns we saw on those first excursions out of Lucca—Borgo a Mozzano, Ghivizzano, Coreglia, Castelnuovo and so on—set the pattern for them all.

That was in the late spring or early summer—it would be hard to say which, for the countryside seemed to lie at the change of seasons.

Lucca lies in the valley of the Serchio River, between Florence and Pisa. But there are ranges of fairly high mountains flanking it on either side; and the highest of these, running up to five or six thousand feet in altitude, still had patches and dribbles of snow showing on their peaks. Yet the hay already was high in the fields we drove through, and poppies glinted blood-red in the grass all along the road. In the first town we stopped at, Borgo a Mozzano, the shop doors all stood open, screened only by the long, varicolored plastic ribbons the Italians use in summer, and the hardware and supply shops were hung, inside and out, with such things as scythes, rakes, sabots, denim work pants and beautifully embossed brass hand spray-tanks—fresh equipment for those who needed it for their work through the growing season ahead.

There was a small, rough-brick church whose two circular

windows above and on either side of the dark oaken portal seemed to stare down at us in sleepy surprise. (These paired round windows, so common among the early Romanesque village churches, I've noticed, often give them an air of innocent wonderment.) And the whole exterior, with its low pent roof and stubby, square bell tower, all warm and brown in the sun, was really quite charming. The interior, unfortunately, had recently been "restored" with the best gilt work and flamboyant Rococo curlicues the town's money could buy; but there was a fine, sturdy thirteenth- or fourteenth-century clock tower over the main portal of such walls as remained which was handsome and well proportioned.

And that about summed up the items of specific esthetic interest in Borgo a Mozzano. For the rest, the town dozed or went lazily about the small, random activities of any country hamlet. Old men sat in pairs talking on the stone benches under the chestnut trees in the graveled piazza, and in the doorways roundabout it women sat mending, knitting or merely gossiping. There were two men chipping away with hammer and chisel at the stuccoed front of one of the houses nearby, I remember. They were in no hurry about it, but it looked as if the work had something to do with resetting a window grating.

Farther on, I stumbled on a charming little street, called the via Delle Loggie, which was almost completely roofed over with a succession of ancient, jutting, half-timbered balconies, their balustrades lined with potted flowers; and beyond that I came upon a tiny stream winding unhurriedly through, with more groups of old men sitting on the low stone walls that contained it.

A few miles above Borgo a Mozzano there is a fork in the road. One fork branches off to the right, following a tributary of the Serchio, a mountain-fed stream called the Lima. This fork is in fact the main road. One of the big truck routes of

Italy, it climbs up past a town called Bagni di Lucca, an ancient watering place whose fame goes back to Roman times and which, much later, was a favorite resort of Elisa Baciocchi during her brief rule as Duchess of Lucca, and then on, still climbing, through huge pine forests and tiny huddled villages to a saddle in the Apennines called the Abetone Pass —from which it slants down and north to Modena and thence on, eventually, to the Brenner Pass at the Austrian frontier.

We kept to the left, that day, still following the Serchio; above the Lima, the whole valley changes considerably in character. We were entering a region called the Garfagnana— but here I must make a brief interpolation, this one on the subject of the Italian landscape, which can vary much more suddenly and radically than is generally realized.

Here again, as in so many other things Italian, there is a standard and somewhat erroneous concept, and it's one whose origins it would be interesting sometime to track down in detail. My guess is, though, that it stems from the French and English Romantic painters, from Claude Le Lorrain and Turner on down to Corot and Whistler, abetted by their poet-contemporaries, who "discovered" Italy successively in the eighteenth and nineteenth centuries.

The French had Rome as their main point of departure; the English had Florence, and between them they concocted an Italy whose main features were a ruined bridge in a wooded glade, with a lone shepherd or, occasionally, a pair of rustic lovers beside the flood, and, above him (or them) a line of poplars etched against a sunset sky—all of which became as much a symbol of Italy as a windmill is of Holland or a pyramid is of Egypt.

These components are there to be found too, especially the line of poplars, if you want to look for them, and in the way that we force nature to imitate art we do seek them out and feel a certain satisfaction in finding them. As a matter of fact, though, the range is a great deal wider than that. Just a few miles south and east of the terraced slopes around Florence, you turn a corner in the road, so to speak, and find yourself on a rolling plateau called the Pratomagno, or Great Plain, which is as bare, tawny and unpopulous as some sections of the Dakotas.

The upper reaches of the Tiber, north of Sansepolcro, are another pocket of desolation in the midst of abundance, while, still farther east, along the old Via Flaminia (we were on our way to Urbino then) the road worries its way through a series of gorges as savage as anything I've seen outside the Rockies —culminating in a one-car-wide tunnel carved through solid rock that dates from Roman times.

Heading south from there, you come into the mountains of the Abruzzi, where the wild boar and the chamois still are hunted. Here you will see not shepherds but goat herders, long-caped and heavy-booted, standing leaning on their staffs, gazing silently down at you from a ledge above the road as you drive past. Goats are about the only animals that can find footing and forage in the region, and the men seem to move about a good deal with their flocks in search of pasture: the slopes are dotted with miserably makeshift huts, built up loosely of piled rocks, chinked and roofed with straw, where they can sleep out on their wanderings.

Father south still, the peaks rise higher, to form the chain called the Gran' Sasso, where Mussolini, reputedly, hid out for a while before making his final, fatal dash for the frontier. Here the mountains are high enough (around eight thousand feet) to hold snow well into the spring. There is a cable-car lift that takes you up to an inn some fifteen hundred feet short of the top, and when we were there, in June, there were still a few hardy souls about who had come up from Rome, only a hundred or so miles away (and already having its first heat wave), for some last minute, catch-as-catch-can climbing and skiing in the snow fields still hanging on at the summit.

Somewhat the same transformation occurs, though in less

spectacular fashion, as one mounts the Serchio. Above its confluence with the Lima, the river dwindles; the valley narrows and its sides become more precipitous, with great rocky spurs reaching fingerlike down from the mountains on either side. The towns—Ghivizzano, Coreglia, Barga, Castelnuovo di Garfagnana, Gallicano; there are literally dozens of them—sit on the spurs, well back from the road and high above it, with the vineyards and olive groves that form their main crops sloping down to the grain fields and hay fields below. Since the valley was a main approach route to Lucca from the north—for pilgrims in the early days of Christianity and for soldiery at all epochs—all are fortified; and the succession of walls and castellations, some in ruins and some more or less intact, add a curious touch of grimness to the whole atmosphere of the valley.

We didn't—we couldn't—visit all the towns, for there were far too many. Ours, too, was a spur-of-the-moment venture, as all such excursions should be.

We did have a guidebook of sorts to start with. It was a paper-bound pamphlet, locally printed, called *Lucca e La Sua Provincia.* I had picked it up at a bookstore a day or two before, and I owe the trip to it—unless it be that I owe it still more to Laurence and the fact that he has a tendency to insomnia. He makes the best of the awkward circumstance by reading—starting with Montaigne, Joinville, Saint-Simon and Rabelais (he had a duffel bag full of such material to start with) and ending, desperately, as the trip continued, with reading anything.

So it happened that, one night at about three in the morning, he turned to *Lucca e La Sua Provincia,* and next morning at breakfast came out with the information that if I was looking for hill towns—especially the less well-known variety—we had a fair-sized assortment ready to hand. Most of them were, in fact, so obscure that he had never heard of them himself—and his knowledge of Italy is as wide and well-founded as mine, in this category at least, was superficial.

We took off the same day to investigate, on the first of what turned out to be many such charming, chancy ventures. Though we followed the guidebook at the start, in the end we more or less discarded it; thenceforward—and this is the best way, at all times—we went along on our own, turning off the main road and onto the inevitably twisting, ascending side one, more or less as the impulse moved us.

As it was, on that first day, I saw so many—all of them, too, so alike in their basic structure—that they tend to run together in my memory, and frequently it is the trivial as much as the important things that recall one or another of them to my mind. I remember Castelnuovo, for example, for its fortifications—and also, oddly enough, for its haystacks.

To be sure, later on and in other sections of Italy, I saw equally small towns that were even more heavily fortified: Radicofani, Poppi, Monteriggione—the last a mere shell of a town now, but a one-time papal stronghold whose towers impressed Dante so much that he used them as a comparison with those guardian giants ringing the pits in the third circle of hell. Castelnuovo, however, was the first whose fortifications I had had the chance to explore, and they certainly were impressive. They are largely in ruins now. But enough remains to show the skill of their planning: the main walls towered at intervals, the towers machicolated, and culminating in a larger donjon or keep which could serve as a final rallying point for the defenders; the whole surrounded by a dry moat or trench, with another escarpment beyond.

As so often happens in Italy, the fortifications have been gradually taken over by the town and incorporated into its fabric. I remember one corner turret that had been converted into an apartment, with its top serving as a balcony. (The view from there must have been magnificent.) Another had been used as the foundation for a church tower, boosting it, so to speak, that much higher toward the sky; and there were several places where the ancient stones, big blocks whose size and the amount of whose weathering suggested an Etruscan origin, had been lifted out bodily to piece out the walls of buildings nearby.

The town itself was a concentration of houses and cobblestoned alleys, rather dark, rather quiet, with little movement at the time we were there in the streets or in the piazza, and to tell the truth I don't remember much about it. In a sense, the walls overshadowed it, and my main memory is of a walk along the floor of the trench, now converted into a cattle path, at the base of the fortifications.

The air there was damp and the feeling somber, for the height of the walls on either side held it in almost perpetual shadow. But the path led to a break in the outer walls and a grassy plot where we sat for a while in the sun, and it was there that I had my first good look at the haystacks—hay houses, really—in the yards of the valley farms below.

Hay is treated with considerable respect throughout Italy, I've discovered. While still curing in the fields, it is raked into neat cross- or rosette-shaped mounds; and the stacks, when made, are if not works of art certainly works of great artisanship. Ordinarily, they are cylindrical, and the hay, as used, is cut off in narrow vertical strips, thus reducing the stack spirally and creating the effect of an extraordinarily tall chambered nautilus, un-growing instead of growing.

Here, however, in the Garfagnana, the stacks—if that is the word for them—were constructed in the form of actual houses, the walls vented here and there with openings that looked like windows and the whole surmounted by a V-shaped thatching that served both as roof and as protection against the weather; and the effect, as I looked down on them from above, was at once childlike, slightly ridiculous and utterly charming.

Unfortunately, I never saw one of the hay houses in process of construction; wherever we went, we seemed always to be in the wrong season for that. As the summer wore on, though, I did see them in various stages of demolition—as the hay, like the gingerbread in the old witch's house in *Hansel and Gretel*, was taken off to feed the cattle. It was delightful to note how carefully the basic form was preserved, diminishing from house to bungalow size, then to playhouse and finally down almost to doll-house dimensions.

So it went all through our leisurely trip up the Serchio. We had lunch at a little trattoria outside Barga, or was it Gallicano? One does stumble on fine examples of art in these towns, and you appreciate them the more because they are unexpected. The church at Gallicano, I remember, has an unusually fine Della Robbia altarpiece—but so, for that matter, has the one at Barga. Once they had perfected their marvellous glaze, the Della Robbias, father, nephew and sons (there were seven of them altogether), went into what almost amounted to mass production, and their relatively inexpensive but invariably attractive bas-reliefs and other pieces are as much a fixture in the lesser churches of Italy as Rogers Group sculptures used to be on Victorian mantels.

The lunch, too, was excellent: the swirled egg-drop soup called stracciatelli, followed by a bistecca of veal (the Italians use veal interchangeably with beef for broiling, and the veal is frequently better) which the proprietor-chef, in true country fashion, brought out for our inspection before putting it on the fire; and a local cheese and a salad which could hardly have been fresher, for one of the daughters skipped out to the kitchen garden and picked the lettuce for it while we were engaged with the meat.

The wine, again a local product, was good too, and the setting, a table under a trellis beside the inn, was practically idyllic. It made me feel that life in the hill towns, for all their isolation, had its compensations. But which town was it? I can't remember.

I remember Ghivizzano, though, both for its magnificent view out over the Serchio valley and for a sidelight I got on the hill villages in general. There is, after all, a certain mystery about them. For one thing, there is little—little, that is, that is easily discoverable—in the way of individual history behind them, any more than there is behind the majority of similar small, isolated farm communities in this country.

In the region where I live, on the New York State side of the Berkshires, we are lucky in having a lady, named Mrs. Frank Rundell, whose memory is as long as it is retentive and who writes entertainingly in our newspaper, the *Chatham Courier*, about old times in the vicinity. In Radicofani, down below Siena, I ran across a young fellow named Mario Rappuoli, a poet, who had written a small treatise on the town's history. In another, a town called Alviano, not far from Assisi, I got to talking with the local representative of the Ministero dei Lavori Pubblici—the Italian equivalent of our Public Works Administration, and a godsend to these villages when the economic going gets rough—who knew a good deal about *his* town's background.

For the most part, though, the history of such towns is almost as veiled as the dark past they have their roots in,*

---

* In contrast, incidentally, with the wealth of information we have about Imperial Rome. When we were in Rome, we were taken by an archaeologist acquaintance to a museum called the Museo della Civiltà Romana, located in a huge and rambling, three- or four-storied building halfway out the via Ostiense, on the via Tre Fontane, which is simply filled with relics of life in the days of the Empire. These are casts, or reproductions of other sorts, in most cases, for the collection was meant principally for students and archaeologists. But their range is from reconstructions of shops, warehouses, factories, furnishings and all the other minutiae of daily life to a full-size cast of the towering Trajan's Column. The column still stands, of course, in the Piazza Colonna in downtown Rome, but the cast of it is here laid down lengthwise in sections, in a tunnel-like room of its own, so the long, spiraling triumphal

and one of the things that puzzled me was the size of their
fortifications, which seemed totally disproportionate to their
needs. On the face of things, their very location seemed to
make them almost impregnable, except by blockade—and
blockade, to the volatile Italian mind, was too tedious a business to get into, especially against so relatively small a prize.

It was the Romans who excelled at that. They were engineers first and last, every soldier a sapper as much as a fighter,
and there is something terrifying in the accounts of the way
in which they reduced a city: first ringing it with armed
camps and then ringing the camps with earthworks—in effect, constructing a city around a city—and then, well settled
in place and with all the time in the world for the operation,
moving forward their battering rams and their mining equipment, all well covered and well protected and all advancing
slowly, inexorably, towards the final breaching of the walls
and the capture.

There seems little doubt, in my mind at least, that the re-
treat to the hill towns began, possibly as early as Etruscan
times, as a defense against such maneuvers. It's impossible to
undermine a wall that is built on rock, and difficult to use
catapults or battering rams—the heavy artillery of the day—
on a twenty- or thirty-degree slope. Full blockade was the only
way of effecting surrender, and as I've said this didn't seem to
fit the medieval mind. Fashions change in war as in everything else; the sword, the lance and the shock of hand-to-hand
conflict was by then more attractive, and the smaller towns
were merely bypassed or, more often, reduced from within. It

---

procession which is carved on it from top to bottom can be studied at
close hand. The culminating feature of the museum is a scale model of
the city itself, some thirty-odd feet in diameter, with all its streets and
fora, houses, villas and palaces laid out as they were in Augustan times.
It's a half-day's work, at least, just getting through the place, but I
found it well worth it. I did regret, though, that no research even faintly
comparable to this has been done on Medieval or even Renaissance
times.

occurs to me that a good deal of the fiercely destructive factional warfare that went on *inside* the Italian towns may have been, indirectly, the result of their relative security from without.

I can't help feeling, in short, that a good deal of their strenuous fortification was partly a continuation of an old, largely tribal tradition—reaching back, indeed, to the days when there was no such thing as a neighbor and every stranger was automatically an enemy—and partly a matter of mere prestige: other towns, San Gimignano, for example, has a forest of castellated towers, why can't we? In a back-handed sort of way, Ghivizzano confirmed my thesis.

Ghivizzano, even for a hill town, is a steep town. One goes up, up, up—from the valley floor through an alley of plane trees and then up a switchback road to the gates; up again to the main piazza and up farther to a smaller one, a sort of promenade or luogo, really, built out over an arc of the fortifications. It was dedicated, I noticed, not to the fallen heroes of the wars of the Guelphs and Ghibellines, but to the Caduti della Guerra 1915-18, and it was pleasantly grassed and treed. (We had parked the car by then, and were walking; by this time the exertion of the climb had induced a certain urgency: we felt like skirmishers, swarming up a redoubt.)

There was a church on the upper piazza, but the church was closed. It was still siesta time, and the town was dozing. But there was a barred gate beside the church and beyond it a garden and a path, leading up. We went up, of course. We had to ring for a custodian, and the custodian turned out to be a truly rosy-cheeked young priest, the curate of the church below. There had been a sign too, at the gate, a *cave canem*, warning visitors to beware of the dog. But the dog, a police-dog puppy, turned out to be as friendly as the priest; with him rollicking along beside us we went on, still up, through the curate's small vegetable garden to the ultimate eminence of Ghivizzano, a watchtower a few hundred yards above and beyond the church.

We went up, again, to the parapet, and the view from there, as I've said, was magnificent. Just below was the town, its ringed spiral of houses packed so tightly that, when seen from above, their red-, yellow- and brown-tiled roofs, mossed and weathered, looked like a patchwork of faded corduroy, with hardly more than a seam's glimpse of the streets and alleys that lay between. Below it, and beyond a ramble of crumbling fortifications still encircling the town, lay the vineyards —the cropped trees that supported the vines looking more than ever like green candelabra, neatly arrayed in rows; the ranked olive trees, still young in leaf, looking each like a tiny explosion of pale-green smoke; and beyond and below them the brief span of grain or hay fields, reaching down to the river.

Across the river, the hills rose again; and here the clouds added their pattern, their shadows lolling in the hollows and lolloping over the ridges: the whole making an almost perfect panorama of sunny abundance. In a way, though, and in a way that I find difficult to describe, our tower made the keynote of the scene. We had come up through three stories, each connected by a stout wooden ladder leading to a trapdoor, and each floor consisting of a room about twenty feet square. Each room was embrasured on all sides, with stone benches at either side of the embrasures. Each floor had a fireplace, too, and the fireplaces, though small, had been well put together and were probably still serviceable.

It was the coziness of the fireplaces that won me over. These towns, as I've said, were farm towns, and farmers are generally peaceable people, concerned mainly with their crops in their seasonal rotation. If they were going to stand watch, for Guelphs or Ghibellines, for Guinigi or Medici or whomever—and lose the care of their crops in the process—

they were damn well going to make themselves comfortable while doing it. Our tower, I had noticed, bore the squared-off crenellations that proclaimed it to be Guelph, and looking out from the parapet I could see another tower, just a bit farther up the river. It was only a couple of kilometers away, but it was still far enough so that I couldn't quite make out whether it was Guelph or Ghibelline. I've no doubt that the Ghivizzanans knew well enough, in the early days. But I had a sudden feeling that it couldn't have bothered them much, even then.

Cathedral Town

On the face of things, there was some excuse for staying as long as we did—a full week—at Assisi but there seemed no reason on earth for staying even longer at Orvieto. Assisi, architecturally, is among the most elegant of all the hill towns; and the way it lies, its streets looped necklacelike in gradually ascending curves around its hilltop, and with the curves threaded through with innumerable small lanes and byways, makes it an endlessly beguiling place to wander about in.

Orvieto, by contrast, is grim. The general tone of its houses, built of stone taken from the brown, tufalike rock found roundabout, is coffee-colored, while Assisi's, quarried on nearby Mount Subiaco, is an almost uniformly pale, lovely coral. Orvieto, too, is tighter and more constricted in pattern. Henry James, in one of his travel essays, describes a certain "shipboard feeling" that takes hold of some visitors in Italy. He was speaking particularly of Venice; and it's true that in Venice the streets, always shying imperceptibly away from the direction in which you think they are leading you (when they aren't dead-ending suddenly in canals), are admirably designed to bring you back to the very spot you started from, or, conversely, lead you to the Zatteria and the lagoon when you are aiming for the Rialto—in either case, leaving you with the helpless impression of being hemmed in and surrounded by water.

In Orvieto, one is likely to feel islanded, too—not in water, however, but in empty air, and so, in a sense, doubly stranded. For if Assisi excels in the elegance of its design, Orvieto is surely one of the most dramatic, since the whole town lies packed in on the top of a giant upthrust of rock, as round almost as a piston and equally sheer-sided, some six hundred and fifty feet above the broad floor of the valley around it. When it is seen from a distance, and from whatever side and no matter how many times one sees it, sitting there like some stranded galleon, its rust-colored sides topped mastlike by the spires of the great cathedral, the effect is unfailingly breath-taking, and there is something oceanic about the atmosphere of its interior too.

There are times in America when, driving along some road in duny country, one sees one more dune ahead and knows somehow, instantly, from its very outline, that there is *nothing* beyond it—nothing, that is, but the sea; and there were many times similarly in Orvieto when I would see a street-ending before me and realize that the last houses in the double row along it were the *last* houses: there was nothing beyond them but the sky.

Orvieto is, I think, unique among the hill towns in that it has no walled fortifications; its precipitous location takes care of that, and one of the pleasanter features of the place is that the ending-in-air streets like the ones I've just described often finish in a tiny parked space, fitted out with benches and trees and of course automatically supplied with a splendid view—or, occasionally, lead one to a little lane, low-fenced, that leads you meanderingly along the very edge of the cliffs.

Orvieto is not the only town in Italy to have a funicular railway, though I was told so. There is at least one more that we came upon—in Bèrgamo, farther north—and there may be others.* But certainly Orvieto is the place that needs such a contrivance most. There are still only two main roads leading up into it, and although they are well paved and graded now, they go winding around the cliffs in a curiously confusing series of spirals; early diarists, writing in the days of dirt roads and horse-drawn diligences, speak unanimously of the seemingly endless journey required to just simply get *into* the town.

As a result, the funicular, a neat little arrangement of two gray-painted, ferociously stream-lined, mutually balancing cars which runs up from the Rome-Florence railway below—a good part of the way through a slanting tunnel, or shaft, cut in the solid rock—is heavily patronized; and the region around its upper terminus, at the eastern end of the town, is the center of what little new building is going on—most of this so brand-new, so brightly painted and aggressively "modern" in design that we began thinking of it as the "Floral Heights" section of Orvieto.

---

* Orvieto does have a few other unquestioned singularities, though. It was there that the first official "monte di pietà" in Italy—pawnshop, we would say, more vulgarly—was opened. This was set up under Pius II, around 1460, after a Church decision that no sin, "even venial," appertained to the lending of money at interest. Operated by the Franciscans, it was so successful at adding to the Order's revenues that the thing turned into a landslide, with others opening shortly at Perugia, Assisi, Mantua, Parma, Lucca and elsewhere. In Madrid, so I have read, a priest, more than usually hard-pressed for cash, no doubt, to keep even with his church's expenses, started one with a few coins from his alms box, and made it prosper.

Orvieto is also, so far as I know, the only place to have a church now functioning as a garage. This is the former Sant'Agostino, at the edge of the old quarter of the town. It is desanctified now, of course, but its extremely Rococo interior is largely intact, and it was odd indeed to see all the gilt and marble wall curlicues towering above the cars and car parts strewn about the floor.

I've a theory, incidentally, that not enough critical attention is paid to art forms in their debasement, for it's there,
if ever, that their intrinsic flaws are most clearly revealed.
As its insufficient concern with formal structure led to Im-
pressionism's decay, so the stress on sheer practicality of the
"machine for living" Functionalist school has led, in its
commoner or suburban-type manifestations, to a kind of glittering sterility. The Italians, in Orvieto and elsewhere, jazz
their "modern" up a lot, camouflaging it with bands of red,
green and blue paint, adding jutting balconies and so on, but
even so the boxlike barrenness of the structure shows through.

Orvieto is a tough-spirited town, too, one that goes about
its affairs in a rather brusque, jostling, take-it-or-leave-it fashion. Its white wines are its principal product. They are famous for their quality, and deservedly so. Dry and clean, a
bit tangy in flavor but never acid or sharp, they are delicious
and we enjoyed them. There come moments, though, when
a person's taste turns toward a red wine, a Barolo, say, or a
Bardolino—and can one get them in Orvieto?

It was typical of the Orvietans' temper that the answer was
almost invariably no. You took the local white—and paid
handsomely for it, too, for the prices in Orvieto, it seemed
to me, were generally high—or you took nothing; in the end,
we made a sort of game of the matter, trying to find a
restaurant where a decent red wine could be had.

Why, then, in view of all this, did we stay? One reason, I
think, was plain laziness—or, to put a slightly more positive
face on things, it was from a desire just to *be* somewhere for a
while. Touring Italy in one's own car, as we were doing, has
many advantages, most of them revolving around the obvious
fact that you can go where you want when you want to. But
this mobility can become a handicap, too. It's not only
that you find yourself traveling too far and too fast, moving
on from one place to another without pausing long enough
to get to know any of them thoroughly. In addition, you are

likely to develop a kind of gypsy mentality, in which the car, like the tinker's cart or the circus caravan, becomes the solid center of existence, the one permanent thing in a world where everything else—towns, museums, churches, restaurants —is transitory. The car is *home*, the cozy, familiar place where even the random accumulation of baggage acquires an accustomed feeling; and it's only when one is in it, and it in motion, that you feel comfortable. It is the hotel, or the succession of them, checked into one day and checked out of the next, that seems strange and unwelcoming.

It was at Orvieto, though, and somewhat mysteriously, that the mood changed. In the first place, we had planned to stay a little longer than usual there. You can "do" the place, if you like, in a single day, or so the guidebooks will tell you. Nagel, for example—breathing a bit hard, to be sure—takes you through it in what figures out to be about an hour of brisk walking, whisking from the Cathedral ("we leave by the right-hand door") down the Corso Cavour, the main street, to the Piazza della Repubblica and on down to the small, completely medieval quarter at the other end of town. But there comes a time, in the lives of even the most unregenerate of gypsies, when some washing and pressing of clothes and similar refurbishing is necessary, and we had picked Orvieto for that and allotted two, maybe three days for it.

This, however, called for a general unloading of the car. Overnight bags just wouldn't do now. The big bags had to be taken out, and the knapsacks that served as soiled clothes hampers; the typewriter, too, and while we were about it we thought some other things might come out, for possible rearrangement. In the end, we unloaded everything, and it occurs to me that this may have been the key to the change in the situation. For the car, thus denuded, lost its homelike quality. It ceased to be a haven, a burrow, and the result was that—as bare inside and out now, and as forlorn, as a car in a used-car lot—it stood, first in front of the hotel, and then in the nearby Piazza del Popolo; next day, when the market fair took over the square and we had to move it, in a garage—while not two or three days but seven, eight and finally ten days passed before we reclaimed it. Our car was a Renault "Dauphine," as small, frisky and companionable as a puppy-dog, and I had already come to love it; I used to look in on it occasionally, just to make sure it didn't feel too abandoned. We stayed on, though, day after day—stayed, indeed, until the Orvietans themselves began to wonder about us—and in the end found the long stay far from unrewarding.

The Cathedral is the chief feature of the town. Begun around 1285, on the site of still more ancient Etruscan and Roman edifices (Orvieto's name derives from the Latin *urbs vetus*, or "old town") the church owes its origin to a miracle, the so-called "miracle of Bolsena," which, according to the legend, occurred in the year 1263, when a priest, celebrating mass at Bolsena, found drops of blood falling from the bread he had consecrated for the ritual sacrifice. Bolsena is a lake town a few miles south and west of Orvieto, and the priest till then had been having doubts about the truth of the doctrine of transubstantiation, which maintains—if I understand the doctrine correctly—that the bread and wine consecrated in the Mass are transformed, by the act of consecration, into the actual flesh and blood of the Creator.

The miracle resolved his doubts, as well it might, and it so impressed the then Pope, Urban IV, when reported to him, that he ordered the construction of a church to be begun forthwith, in commemoration. (Why he had it built at Orvieto instead of Bolsena is again something of a mystery. But Orvieto was already a favorite resort of the Popes and was also, in stormier times, a refuge; and Bolsena, in addition to being militarily less defensible, was in some sense a dependency.)

The Cathedral is thus an exceedingly holy place, to the devout, and the annual Feast of Corpus Domini which celebrates the miracle, though observed throughout Italy, and indeed throughout the world, is celebrated most solemnly there. Architecturally, the church is generally considered, along with that of Siena (which it much resembles) as the finest example of the Gothic style in Italy. I have my reservations about that, these mainly revolving about all Italian Gothic. Otherwise, I must say that its reputation is deserved.

Its site—though there may be many who will disagree with me about this—is to my mind an advantage. A great church can have as its main approach a vast open square, as with Notre Dame in Paris, in which case the massiveness of the structure is stressed; or, as is the case, most beautifully, with Chartres Cathedral, it can stand hemmed in by the humbler housing of its own period—and then the surroundings soften its might a little, lending a benign, almost partriarchal quality to the general impression. The imposing effect of Chartres is not reduced in any sense by its position. The fact that one has to stand close to it and look up and up and up at the great, gray, towering face of it only adds to its impressiveness. Added too, though, is a certain homeliness, softening the mass and forcing one's attention on the details: one takes it in bit by bit, and gradually.

Orvieto's site is much like Chartres'. It too stands on a smallish square, knee-deep, so to speak, in more or less contemporary thirteenth- and fourteenth-century housing, of which the blocky Palazzo Papale and the larger Palazzo Faina are the most imposing; except for these, it looks down on a row of broad-eaved, low-roofed dwellings that have almost the look of farm cottages.

As with Chartres too, it is almost impossible to get an overall view of it. One stands too close for that; here again the attention is drawn instead to the details, and in this respect Orvieto profits more from its situation than Chartres does, for in Orvieto the details are paramount, from the beautiful filigreelike bas-reliefs on the columns flanking the doors at the base of the structure to the cusped and crocketed spires that surmount it.

Because of our long stay in the town, I had plenty of time to inspect the details of the Cathedral at leisure. I did this mostly from the terrasse of a smallish restaurant just across from it, on the Piazza. It was called, not very imaginatively, the Ristorante Cucina Tipica, or Local Cooking Restaurant, but it did stock red wines as well as white and the food was better than passable. More than that, the proprietor, a thin, nervous, dark-eyed man who doubled as chef, liked good music; instead of the juke box or radio almost inevitable in such places, he had a hi-fi set with an excellent collection of records, and for this reason particularly the Cucina Tipica soon became our favorite dining place in Orvieto.

Best of all, though, in my view, was the fact that it was an unhurried place. This was true, I think, not only because at the time we were there it was only sparsely patronized. In or out of season, in the smaller towns especially, the Italian waiters have a way of serving you as if their lives depended on getting you fed as quickly as possible. It is not that they want to get rid of you, either; I'm convinced that there is no such feeling.

It is rather a part of their desire to please you, coupled with a concern about the food itself; and since everything moves faster in Italy, including the cooks, if your coteletto is ready in the kitchen before you've quite finished with the pasta, and the waiter knows it, you are likely to find him hovering anxiously a few paces behind you—ready, the instant you put your fork aside, even temporarily, to snatch the plate away and, deftly, substitute the one bearing the next course.

There was a restaurant just next door to our hotel in Orvieto which we ended by avoiding for that reason. It was called the Ristorante Ancora—meaning, depending on the placing of the stress, either "The Anchor" or "The Again," and I never discovered which. The food was good, and it had tables outside, where one could eat, in pleasant weather, on a shrubbed, trellised terrace. But the waiter, a thin, nervous boy of only about fifteen, was a demon for speed. He moved at a trot to begin with, and the shrubs gave him a further advantage. He could hide behind them, with the result that one never saw him till—pounce!—the plate you were lingering over was whisked away.

I shall not soon forget the look on Laurence's face when, lunching one day at the Ancora, he laid his fork down to fill out a description of something or other with a gesture, and saw his barely touched omelette vanish straightaway. For all his continental upbringing, Laurence is still an old-line Rhode Islander in his background, and at the moment it happened all his New Englander's feeling about haste and waste came surging to the surface.

He reared back in stony horror. "But I was going to *eat* that!" he cried.

Incidentally, the youth of the lad had no bearing on the matter. Running a restaurant, in Italy, is a family business, and the children start early—and eagerly too—to learn the trade. It was in Venice, in a little restaurant just off the Campo San Barnabas, that we ran across the prize example of this sort of precocity. The waiter in this case was a boy of scarcely seven years, and the fact that he was there at all, we thought, was mainly a sign of paternal indulgence—encouraging him in his budding ambition—for we noticed that he waited only on a few people who were obviously habitués of the place, and his father, the chef, kept glancing out of the kitchen to watch him fondly.

But small as he was, he was dressed in a well-cut waiter's jacket and neatly pressed waiter's black pants, and as he trotted back and forth between kitchen and table he held his arms bent at the elbow and slightly akimbo, in proper waiter's fashion. The night we were there, the effect was marred, deplorably, by a little girl, still younger, who fell in love with him at first sight and kept following him around, entranced, speechless with admiration, and—no matter how fiercely he glared at her—totally unshakable.

I seem to have wandered. But the point is that the pace at the Cucina Tipica was more leisurely, and in consequence we breakfasted there occasionally, as a change from the colazione served at the hotel, and lunched and dined there frequently. Evenings, since there was little else to do in Orvieto, anyway, we often stayed on and on, over a second and sometimes a third or fourth bottle of wine. Our waitress was a plump, dark-haired, round-faced gentle girl called Vanna, a niece of the proprietor, and no matter how long we hung on she would stay on too, uncomplainingly. It wasn't till we discovered, inadvertently, that when it got *quite* late the sound of a motor, revving up and down, outside on the Piazza del Duomo, was the sign that her boy friend was waiting there patiently or impatiently to take her home or for a spin down to the lake resorts around Bolsena on his motor scooter, that we decided it was only the part of decency to curtail our evening vigils a little.*

---

* I can't help adding, as one of the most trivial of items for the formality of a footnote, that the name of the house pet at the Cucina Tipica, a mixed-breed terrier of very friendly disposition, was "Dog."

"Dog?" we repeated when Vanna told us. "But what's his *name?*"

"*Si chiame* 'Dog,' " she said again; and the proprietor, going over his accounts at a corner table—he was always going over his accounts, worriedly, in the evenings—looked up from the pile of papers long enough to corroborate her. "Dog," he told us.

And always—morning, noon and evening—was the Cathedral just across the way from us. As a result, by the time we were ready to leave Orvieto, I had achieved a degree of friendly familiarity with the structure that made it possible for me to see it without even looking at it—if I may put the thing so—and when I did look at it, I could be content with a glancing gaze, letting my eyes linger here or there as the feeling of the moment dictated.

As I suppose was inevitable, I ended with mixed impressions about it—my familiarity breeding, not contempt, but annoyance certainly with a few of its features, sheer delight in a good many others, and both fondness and respect for the whole of the undertaking. I was irked especially by the truly Italian instinct for garishness which had prompted the inclusion of mosaics—and such bad ones too!—in every available corner and angle of the façade, thus obscuring the tiered simplicity of the basic design. Architecturally, too, there are difficulties, for the church as a whole represents an uneasy blending of the Romanesque and Gothic styles, with the Gothic characteristics exemplifying even more clearly than usual the diffidence the Italians seem always to have felt when asked to work in it—the buttressing awkward and unwieldy, the pointed arches serving no sound structural purpose. And from this point of view the façade itself, with its famous rose window, lace-handkerchieflike in the almost incredible delicacy of its stone tracery; and its fluted, flanking columns, its bas-reliefs and other sculptures, its tryptichlike arrangement of the porches enclosing the great main doors—well, handsomely proportioned as it is, isn't it all merely tacked on, more a glittering screen than a real façade, and with no relation to the pure Romanesque character of the interior?

There was something down-to-earth about the Cucina Tipica that fascinated me.

There were times when it seemed so. Yet there is a charm about it that overrides all one's carping. If the true Northern Gothic is essentially a masculine style—as I believe it is: rugged, often a trifle harsh and, even in its aspiringness, wiry and muscular—the Italian treatment may be taken to be the feminine version: slim and light in form, even girlish, while the other is burly. In this sense, the Cathedral at Orvieto may be taken as the ultimate in womanly expression. If she carries her womanliness to the point almost of coquetry there is something winning in her very desire to win you.

The lace-handkerchief window, for all the slight fussiness of its tricked-out, rectangular border, is still beautiful in itself—an almost unbelievably intricate network of stone and glass, set high in the sky above you. The mosaics are a mistake; and the modeling of the whole design of the façade on that of a tryptich was unhappy too, for it condemned it to a kind of formalized angularity from the start.

Still, though, there is a quality that I can only describe as eagerness, a desire to please, about it; and for this reason, perhaps, it is in the very richness of its details that the Cathedral of Orvieto excels. Nowhere else that I know of is there such a profusion of them—put on, more or less as a woman puts on a necklace or a pair of earrings, to attract you.

I might as well start, in my recital, with one of the smallest of them. There are four main columns, each rising to a separate spire, defining the façade. Each is broken by a dozen or more spandrels, and each spandrel is tesselated, from top to bottom, with closely set, diamond-patterned, small, gold tiles. I went over one day, on leaving the Cucina Tipica, and counted the tiles in one section of one of the spandrels. There were thirty of them in the space of one foot of height—and the height went up and up, of course, every foot of it tesselated, and that spandrel was only one-twentieth, perhaps, of the total.

The larger details, in their effect, outweigh the lesser ones.

These are still *added*, in a sense, but hence they are, from one
point of view, more notable: the bronze figures ornamenting
the bases of the spires, and these so curiously "modern" in
concept (I remember particularly an Angel of Death, reading her scroll, that in her attenuations reminded me strongly
of the German Lehmbruck); and the bases themselves, also
in bronze but in bas-relief, depicting various stages of the Old
Testament story, from the Expulsion from the Garden of
Eden to the Last Judgment. . . . All are features that can be
pored over.

Certainly, the people of Orvieto have accepted their Cathedral unreservedly and familiarly, for the great stepped stone
platform on which she stands has become a more than ordinarily popular meeting and lounging place for the townsfolk. Children play bounce ball against the towering side walls
of the nave or go racing about the small piazza; while at all
hours of the day you see the older people congregating in
groups on the steps themselves, not "sunning" themselves—
in the glaring summer heat of Italy no one in his right mind
does that—but *shading* themselves, and moving gradually
from the west to the east side as the Cathedral's shadow, like
that of an enormous sundial, sweeps them along before it.
It all gives, again, a wonderfully villagy quality to the atmosphere.

The interior of the Cathedral is on the whole rather somber,
insufficiently windowed in the Romanesque fashion and
slightly cumbersome in the arrangement of columns and
arches down the nave. For so holy a place it is singularly
lacking in real treasures. There is an enormous reliquary,
done in silver gilt in the fourteenth century by Ugolino di
Vieri, the Sienese master—a triumph of the silversmith's art
certainly, but to my mind almost finicking in the excess of
its ornamentation—which houses the Corporale, as the blood-
stained cloth is called which, supposedly, was in use at the
time the miracle occurred. There are, too, some scattered

frescoes, unfortunately difficult to see in the uneven lighting, by Pintoricchio, Lippo Lemmi and others.

The chief pride of the church itself, however, is the series of frescoes called "The Last Judgment," by Luca Signorelli, which fill the Cappella Nuova, in one of the transepts. Signorelli is not, I believe, much represented in this country, and he seems generally to be regarded as a transitional figure, important principally because he bridges the gap between the calm, humanistic Classicism of Piero della Francesca (whose pupil for a time he was) and the surging Neo-Classicism, Romantic in mood, of Michelangelo—who, in turn, was certainly influenced by him.

I had already come across some Signorellis in Cortona, a town only twenty miles or so south of Arezzo, where we had been staying at the time. Cortona was Signorelli's birthplace, and it was also the place where he spent the last years of his fairly long life. (He was born in the decade between 1440 and 1450, and died in 1525, so his life span was anywhere from seventy-five to eighty-five, pretty good in either case. When we talk about the miserably low life expectancy of the men of the Middle Ages, as compared to now, it is chiefly of the statesmen, prelates and warriors we are speaking. The artists—with Tintoretto living to be seventy-six, Titian into his nineties and so on—averaged pretty well. It is only in modern times that artists have become less long-lasting than men of affairs.)

The paintings at Cortona, to come back to them, were not impressive. Signorelli, by the very fact of being transitional, had varying fortunes in the course of his career: considerable success in his middle years, when he appeared to have brought the new science of perspective, first projected by Piero, Uccello and others of that generation, to an unheard-of (and indeed it now seems almost mechanical) pitch of perfection; and then a decline afterward, when he was overshadowed by

such newcomers of greater genius as Raphael and Michelangelo.

He seems to have been philosophical about it. Gathering
what glory remained to him, he retired to his native Cortona,
where he was bound to bulk larger than he had in Rome or
Florence, and in fact he ended his days there, cheerfully
turning out altarpieces, predellae and other works, to local
order.

There's no question, however, that the "Last Judgment"
at Orvieto, done in the beginning years of the sixteenth century, when he himself was in his fifties, is his masterpiece.

Signorelli's contract for its execution is still extant, dated
April 15, 1499. In it, he agrees to complete the ceiling for
two hundred ducats, and the walls for six hundred more; he
is also to be supplied with suitable lodgings in the town while
he is engaged on it, together with a ration of two measures of
wine and two quintals of grain per month. A quintal was
fifty kilos or about a hundred pounds, and a ducat is, I believe, taken to have been worth about three dollars in gold,
though it is always difficult to estimate real values in terms of
present prices. I don't know what a "measure" of wine con-
sisted of, though I'm sure Signorelli did, for according to all
accounts he liked good living.

But whatever the total may have been it was a bargain,
both for the Church and for posterity. It took him three
years to complete it, working off and on, and I shan't try to
describe it in detail; there are too many reproductions available. Cast in six large panels, plus a number of small medal-
lions and other decorative items—the whole filling the greater
part of one wing of the Cathedral transept—it is too big for
such treatment. Besides, it is not in its step-by-step, descrip-
tive qualities, but rather in the overall concept, that it excels.

What Signorelli undertook here was the truly grandiose
idea of picturing the actual end of the world. (It occurs to me
that the same subject preoccupies us now, but for different

causations, and we approach it mainly through the medium of science fiction. Both are mystical.) The range, therefore, from Signorelli's point of view, goes on from the mere physical destruction—not a nuclear, but here a kind of fulminative explosion—through the even more awful spiritual events that followed: the coming of the Anti-Christ and his defeat; the Judgment, and the division of the Elect from the Damned; to, finally, the Resurrection.

Here, the times were on Signorelli's side. The old, physical, hellfire-and-brimstone conception of life and of death was ending. The Age of Enlightenment was dawning; and as far as I know Signorelli was the last man, or the last artist at any rate, to depict the whole panorama of the holocaust— the bloated Anti-Christ (whose coming was even then being predicted by the gloomy followers of Savonarola), the beatification of the Saved and the horrid Dantesque punishments of the Damned—with an equal degree of both vividness and conviction.

The work has its faults—these residing mainly in a certain, almost metallic harshness of color, a coldly linear quality of design, and above all an excessive exploitation of the "naturalistic" properties of perspective drawing. But as one stands in the chapel, surrounded by the swarming, struggling figures, one can't help but be impressed by the might of the conception. It is easy to understand that when it was completed, in 1505, it created a sensation throughout Italy; and easy, too, to believe the story that Michelangelo, even then committed to the execution of the Sistine Chapel, similar in conception, made a special journey to see it. It's not hard, either, to accept the theory that Michelangelo's famous *terribilità* was at least presaged by the awesomeness of Signorelli's chapel at Orvieto.

There are other points of interest in Orvieto. The sense of age is relative; and the American, accustomed to feel that

New Bedford, Massachusetts, is an "old" town, and that Williamsburg, Virginia, reconstructed as it is, is truly ancient, often finds it hard to get used to the fact that a place like Orvieto—almost all of which dates from the thirteenth to the fifteenth century—has a quartiere vecchio, or "old quarter," which is even older.

There it is, though, in the south end of town, opposite the Cathedral quarter, and it *is* older—a tangle of narrow streets and threadlike alleys, all circling, swirling almost, around a couple of churches, San Giovanni and San Giovenale, of which the latter, a hunched little structure—low-roofed, brown-walled and squat-towered—dating from the very beginning of the eleventh century and now looking as if shrunken with age in the clutter of houses around it, is the more interesting.

The Etruscan collection in the Palazzo Faina is one of the finest in Italy, and it is made up also almost entirely of objects found in the immediate locality. For Orvieto is really an old town, older even than the Quartiere Vecchio: even in Etruscan times it is believed to have been a holy place, and there is an Etruscan necropolis at the base of the cliffs, recently unearthed—the tombs in rows like heavy-roofed stone hovels, in the Etruscan fashion, and dank even on a summer day with the musty scent of antiquity—which is surely worth a visit.

But all these are listed in the guidebooks, and as they will tell you Orvieto can be covered conveniently in a day or so. What the guidebooks leave out is the life of a town and its people. As we stayed on and on there, the grim, brown place came alive around us, acquiring warmth and individuality. My wife bought flowers regularly for our hotel room, and in that way we got to be friends with the chambermaid, a slight, lively creature whose name, it turned out, was Fiorella, or Little Flower, and who scurried upstairs and down collecting vases big enough to hold the supply. The proprietor, forbidding at first, thawed considerably too. He was a tall, bony man, with a long, doubting nose and a heavy-lidded, sidelong glance, and like all the other Orvietans he wondered about us.

We were fixtures by then. Bus tours and motor travel have changed the character of tourism in Italy. People nowadays make their headquarters in Rome, let's say, or Florence, and make side excursions from there; if they stay, if they stay at all, in a place like Orvieto, it's for overnight at most, and more often merely for lunch. By now, the population of our little hotel had changed a half-dozen times. We had seen a busload of basketball players come and go, as well as countless smaller contingents of German, English and American tourists. (Basketball is becoming a popular sport in Italy, and this group had come from Ferrara to compete with the Orvietan team, in a tournament organized by *Il Messaggero* of Rome, as I recall it. They were swaggering youths, wearing shorts and pullovers all the time in spite of the fairly cool weather. But as an adopted Orvietan I am happy to say that they left defeated.)

I remember, too, a covey of nuns who arrived to spend a night there. They were all young, perhaps novices in fact, except for a couple of older nuns who had them in charge, and they were on some sort of pilgrimage to the Cathedral. But it was an outing for them, nonetheless, and I still remember how they flitted back and forth from one to another's room, giggling and chattering (nuns, by virtue of the secludedness of their habitual life, tend to go all girlish when released from it), and kept running downstairs to the sweets shop around the corner for supplies of ice-cream cones and other gelati—until the older nuns succeeded in herding them all off to bed at last.

Next day, they were gone. We remained, and the padrone finally gave voice to his wonderment about us, and began sounding us out guardedly about our lengthy visit. I still re-

Monteriggione—the sad, shut little chapel.

Radicofani—the town chapel. Brown and blank outside, it houses an unusually handsome group of Della Robbia altarpieces.

(Above) Monteriggione—*the big, bare, sandy piazza, and you can see why we decided not to lock the car. But why are all the oxen in Italy white?*

(Below) Arezzo—*the Piazza Grande, sloping down from the charming, trinkety Palazzo della Misericordia to the stately colonnaded apse of Santa Maria della Pieve.*

(Right) Arezzo—*the arcades of the mercato on the uphill side of the Piazza Grande—and how cool and spacious they must have seemed to the two young soldiers.*

San Gim
Piazza d

San Gimignano—the steps to the Museo Civico, left of the Cathedral. A man hurrying somewhere.

igh noon, no market, and the
a almost deserted.

*Orvieto—about eleven a.m. on the Piazza
del Duomo, on the still shady side of the
Cathedral. Taken from the Cucina Tipica.*

(Above) Orvieto—*the cottages across from the Cathedral.*
(Below) Orvieto—*nearly every day is market day at Orvieto, in the Piazza del Popolo—and an unusually crowded and lively market it is!*

(Right) *Market day again—this time in Assisi. Here the market straggles **a** little, climbing up the side streets from the Piazza del Commune.*

Alviano—as seen from the via Tiberini—and one of the rare instances when you look down on a hill town, instead of up.

call how he hooted when my wife, in perhaps a trifle too enthusiastic a tone, told him we *liked* Orvieto; it was *una bella città.*

"*Orvieto bella?*" he cried, and shook his head vigorously. Orvietans are nothing if not realistic, and we weren't fooling him for a minute.

"*Antica, si!*" he went on. "*Ma bella, no!*"

I finally told him I found it a good place to get some writing done, which was partly true.

We were fixtures at the Cucina Tipica too, and there were other places roundabout where the uniform brown of the town was illuminated, metaphorically, like a map with bright-colored pegs placed in it here and there, by the warmth of recognition. We were friends with the lean, impeccably dressed, elderly Italian who ran the florist shop on the Corso Cavour—ran it, so to speak, by remote control, for he spent most of the day sitting on a bench across the street from it, conferring with his cronies, while his wife and daughter did the selling.

We were friends—or I, at least, was a devoted admirer— of the lovely pale, oval-faced girl who sat like a caged angel behind her wicket at the post office, and guided me patiently through the intricacies of getting proofs, manuscripts and other such fairly weighty matter off to the States, air mail, without quite going broke in the process.

We were friends—as with the others, in passing, of course —with Girardo, the manager of the garage where we kept the car, who loved to practice his English on us whenever we took it out; and there were others—waiters, shopkeepers, people unnamed and unknown, who took to bowing or smiling (Orvieto is a small town) as we passed them in the streets or encountered them in a caffè.

I don't know if they miss us; in fact, I'm sure they don't. But in that dim, evanescent way that is the way of travelers, I miss them.

Art In—and Out of—Situ

We stayed longest at Aosta, Lucca, Arezzo, Orvieto and Assisi, among the hill towns. But between-times we made a number of side trips—some planned and, in a not too determined sort of way, purposeful; some completely spur-of-the moment—to other, usually smaller towns, most of them either in Umbria or in Tuscany. We drove over to Cortona one day from Assisi, for example, more or less on the trail of the fifteenth-century painter Luca Signorelli, whose "Last Judgment" in Orvieto I've just described. Or that was, at any rate, the excuse for a day's outing—as, on another day, we made a visit to the birthplace of Raphael the excuse for a trip farther north to the town of Urbino.

Cortona was Signorelli's birthplace, and it was also his place of retirement, for as I've said before he went back in his last years and died there; and though the paintings of his that are still in the town turned out to be a disappointment the trip itself—across the valley of the Tiber, a smallish stream here, and up to Perugia; down again to skirt the weedy, sullen-looking shores of Lake Trasimeno (where, one bloody June morning close to twenty-three centuries ago, in fog, Hannibal all but wiped out the Roman army of thirty-odd thousand men sent against him) and then up again, more and more steeply, to the high, slanting perch of Cortona—this was pleasant and varied enough to make up the difference.

I'd got interested in Signorelli after seeing his master-piece, the frescoes of the Resurrection and Judgment Day in the Cappella Nuova of the cathedral at Orvieto, but in an odd way it was the man as much as the artist that intrigued me. The paintings themselves, huge in scale and daring in con-cept as they are—and pivotal, too, in the history of art—are primarily literary and philosophic accomplishments. In the sense that they evoke no compelling emotional response—and no feeling, either, that the artist was himself emotionally involved—they are illustrations rather than creations.

But the man was pivotal in another sense too, for he came at a time when the painter was gradually emerging from the status of an artisan into that of the true "artist," and by his love of fine living—Vasari remarks that he lived "more in the manner of a nobleman than that of a painter"—he un-questionably helped along the transformation. There's a self-portrait, incidentally, in a lower corner of one of the Orvieto frescoes, where he shows himself standing with Fra Angelico, surveying the painted scene. Fra Angelico was the man orig-inally commissioned to decorate the chapel, so the inclusion is a generous gesture. But the contrast between the older man's simple monk's robe and cowl and Signorelli's jaunty furred cap, richly folded robe and generally fashionable at-tire is so ostentatious as almost to rob the gesture of its graciousness. Even his pose is a trifle swaggering.

Yet Vasari admired, even loved him, as did most of his contemporaries, speaking of his kindness, gentleness and con-sideration; and certainly he seems to have accepted his de-cline in importance philosophically. No longer offered the big commissions, he settled down quite contentedly to the lesser ones, the altarpieces and so on, which he turned out with his apprentices in a workshop he had in Cortona.

In that carefree way the Renaissance art patrons had in dealing with men who had gone out of favor, a good many of these works, I believe, have been painted over or otherwise lost sight of; and as I've said, and as I'd half expected, the ones that remain in Cortona are not among his best examples.

There's an altarpiece of his, a "Virgin with Two Saints" in the Church of San Domenico, just outside the town walls, and another, together with a fresco, in San Nicolo, higher up inside the town; and there are a couple of other pieces, most notably a strongly composed "Descent from the Cross," in the local museum, called the Museo Diocesano. (Signorelli was certainly industrious.)

But his style had by then become harsher and the treatment a trifle repetitive. Only his superb skill as a draftsman remained, and on the whole I liked better a lovely little "Virgin and Child" by Sassetta; and an even more exquisite "Annunciation" by Signorelli's part-time partner, Fra Angelico, where the two bent heads of the angel and the Virgin, the play of their hands—the whole pose, in fact—convey an almost breathless atmosphere of momentousness and adoration.

Cortona itself, however, in its quiet, somewhat out-of-the-way, provincial fashion, turned out to be charming. Though it's just off the main route through Perugia to Arezzo, and about halfway between the two, it is more deeply enfolded by hills than either of them; and this and the fact that it is a steep town—I remember it as one of the steepest of all the hill towns I went into—combine to give it an air of remoteness and isolation, and the truth is that it is relatively little visited.

Like all the hill towns—those so "like" and yet so astonishingly unlike places—it has a character of its own. But I've learned that one's feeling about such matters can vary according to the individual spectator and his mood of the moment. Henry James called Cortona an "arrogant little city," for example. But James could be finicking, and from his account (in his *Italian Hours*) he arrived on a religious feast day, when the churches were crowded and everything else was closed, and he was annoyed by the hubbub around him.

The feast day, it turned out, was in honor of Santa Margherita da Cortona, whose "incorruptible" remains are on view in the church of her name, at the summit of the town. The majority of the early saints were true workers in the faith and, when necessary, sacrificed themselves valiantly for it. Others, though, seem now to have been merely hallucinated, deriving their acclaim from the curious respect the medieval peoples gave to all madmen. Santa Margherita, who lived in the thirteenth century, was one of these. She had visions and is, or was, credited with performing miracles. She also did many good works—such as taking care of orphans, and, at the same time, abandoning her own children. But to say the least she seems to have been an eccentric, going about in rags, subsisting only on table scraps and, in the end, almost literally starving herself to death in pursuit of holiness.

The church, a tenth-century structure that has been restored extensively, and horribly, is as I've said at the very peak of the town. I'd seen similarly miraculously preserved remains before, notably those of Santa Chiara, good San Francesco's friend, at Assisi. There, her face wizened and blackened with time or with exposure, in nun's garb and looking like a dressed-up mummy, the saint's corpse lies in the crypt of her church, the epitome of the Church at its darkest and most medieval.

But Assisi is by definition a reliquary. Cortona is not, and in Santa Margherita's case I just didn't feel up to it. I settled instead for a visit to a charming, small, villagy church just below, San Cristofero, patron saint of lepers and travellers. Brown, brick, clumpily Romanesque in design and set in a small triangular piazza under chestnut and plane trees that seemed almost as venerable as it was, it had at least the virtue of unpretentiousness.

Cortona is also an old town. It was old when Hannibal made his incursion into the valley below it, and its origins are mysterious, though the walls, with their huge foundation stones, indicate that it was an important fortress even in Etruscan times. (The Etruscans, having no knowledge of cement, depended on the size of their building blocks for strength.)

For the rest, I remember it as a kind of gaunt town: not so gaunt architecturally as the still more northerly towns of Gubbio and Urbino, both of which I visited later, nor so uncompromising, but with, along with its aloofness, a certain *waiting* quality, as if the years were at last catching up with it.

A good deal of the character of the hill towns of Italy rests, quite simply, on the color of their buildings—which derives, in turn, from the local stone they are made from. Orvieto is brown, from the tufa deposits around it, and so, for the same reason, is Volterra. Assisi is pink, from the quarries on nearby Mount Subiaco; Urbino, like San Gimignano, is gold. Cortona's stone has a silvery quality, as I recall it. It has the slightly ashen look of age quietly approaching ghostliness.

Almost equally ancient, Gubbio—the town we visited next —is granitic and gray, and a little on the grim side; unlike most of the towns roundabout, it is built on a sidehill instead of a summit, and it is dominated, not by the usual *rocca*, or castle-fortress, but by two fortress-palaces.

These are the Palazzo dei Consoli—the seat of civic power

in the twelfth and thirteenth centuries, when the town was an independent commune and ruled by elective consuls— and the Palazzo Pretorio, or Courthouse. Both face each other across an uncommonly treeless, stone-paved and unattractive piazza, midway up the ascent of the town; and both are built, so to speak, cliff to cliff—with their downhill façades reaching up and up, blankly windowless and unswervingly perpendicular, some sixty to seventy feet from their footing on the steep, rocky slope below to the level of the piazza.

Placed—symbolically, I'm sure—above them is the Palazzo Ducale, built a couple of centuries later when Gubbio, almost ruined by Guelph-and-Ghibbeline internal warfare, passed voluntarily under the suzerainty of the Dukes of Montefeltro. But the Palazzo Ducale—perhaps again symbolically, for the Montefeltri were exceptionally enlightened for their age—is appreciably less menacing in design.

Apart from its ceramics, which have long been a specialty, Gubbio has few pretensions in the way of fine arts. Its main museum possession—and an important one too, archaeologically—is a set of bronze tablets discovered nearby, dating from the fourth century B.C. and called the Iguvine tablets (the town's name, in Latin, was Iguvium), which bear matching inscriptions in Latin and ancient Umbrian, thus affording scholars one of their first clues to the structure of the older tongue.

Otherwise, Gubbio's history was martial from the start. A round thousand Gubbian knights and their men-at-arms joined the First Crusade, and a certain combative atmosphere is part of its heritage still. Its main annual event, far from being a religious festival, is the Palio della Balestra, or Crossbow Contest; and I thought it worth noting that the walls of Gubbio, instead of being scrawled with the political slogans and imprecations commoner elsewhere—"VV [for *Evviva*] Gronchi," "Togliatti—Impostore" and so on—bore more often the inscription "VV Coppi."

The big bicycle marathon called the Gira d'Italia was in progress then, and Coppi was the *campione* "on whose shoulders," as one Italian sports writer put it, "were placed the hopes of all our lovers of the racing wheel." The load may have been more than even Coppi could carry, for in the end he failed to win. A Frenchman named Anquetil did.

Urbino, Gubbio's neighbor to the north, has more artistic attractions; indeed, it has probably the finest museum collection of any of the small towns in Italy.

It may be asked, though—I've often asked it of myself— why one should go so far afield to see paintings or sculptures in their original place—or, as the saying goes, *in situ*. The Metropolitan Museum, for one, has better Raphaels than Urbino has; and certainly the Museum's examples of other artists are far better displayed than a good many of the frescoes and other church paintings we all make our arduous way to, I still remember the guides in the cavernous vaultings of the Lower Church at Assisi, using flashlights (for all the world like the lecturers at the Hayden Planetarium) to point out the details they were talking about of the frescoes there.

Why the bother, then? As a matter of fact, the techniques of color reproduction have been brought to such a point of near-perfection that it's quite possible to study the works of the great masters without going to a museum at all.

The fact is still, though, that a reproduction is not and never will be a painting, any more than even the best recordings are a substitute for live music; and though my argument may be a trifle tenuous logically, about the best way I can describe the difference between seeing a work of art in a museum and seeing it *in situ* is by comparing it to the difference one feels in listening to a recording and in listening to a concert—where the lights, the hushed attendance and the sight of the ranked, rapt musicians, their bows stabbing the air in unison, all contribute to a feeling of being present at the actual *production* of the work.

In the case of a painting, something of the atmosphere surrounding its creation comes through to enrich it. Sansepolcro, unchanged throughout the centuries (if one excepts such manifestations as a cinema here and there and a Singer Sewing Machine agency on the main street), simply breathes of Piero della Francesca. It would be impossible to think of Ravenna's mosaics anywhere but where they are, in Ravenna; and no museum could hope to capture the sense of total immersion in the creative event that one has in the Arena Chapel at Padua, looking at the Giottos there.

Urbino speaks almost as much of its most illustrious ruler, the fifteenth-century Duke Federico da Montefeltro, as it does of its artists; and in a sense the two are intertwined, for he was host and patron during his reign to a long series of painters, from the Fleming Joos van Gent to the most illustrious contemporary Italians.

Federico himself must have been something of a character. Patron of the arts though he was, he was also a warrior, one of the great condottieri, or professional soldiers, of his time; and certainly he was convivial. Unlike his more aloof, or more timid, compeers among the gentry, he is said to have mingled freely with his townsfolk, chatting and drinking, and in his younger days he appears to have been something of a brawler. There's a painting of him in the Ducal Palace at Urbino, now the home of the local museum, which illustrates his divided character: attributed to the Spaniard, Alonso Berruguete, it shows him seated before a lectern placidly reading a book, with his infant son Guidobaldi beside him. But he's clad, a trifle incongruously, in full armor, and the full-fleshed face and short, burly body suggest a man bursting with energy.

Yet he was a man of wide and cultivated interests and, for

his time, magnanimous. At the sack of Volterra in 1472, after
the siege in which he participated as one of the leaders of the
Florentine forces, he asked only, as his share of the booty, a
certain Hebraic manuscript copy of the Bible that he had
coveted, and his library was one of the most celebrated of his
day. Giovanni Santi, Raphael's father (Raphael's baptismal
name was Raffaelo di Sanzio, which may help a little), was
one of his court painters; and when Giovanni died the Duke
generously (for he could hardly have suspected then what
a genius he had in his care) took the boy, then only eleven,
into his household.

Piero della Francesca, late in life, was a guest there, and
so were many others; and it's small wonder, under the circumstances, that the collection the Duke left was a rich one. It is
now—or in this case surely one should say, still—housed in
the Ducal Palace, a vast, round-towered structure, in a series
of spacious, high-ceilinged and now rather bare-looking rooms
meandering around a handsome Renaissance courtyard (including a small retiring room, done in marquetry in the then
popular trompe-l'oeil style, in which the Duke could escape
from his own magnificence; and one of its features that I
couldn't help noting was the inscription over each portal,
from room to room. "FE DUX," it read, incised in gilt letter-
ing, and the guests, by their very passage beneath it, were supposed to have given token proof of their faith and allegiance.

At this distance, there is probably not much point in cataloguing too thoroughly the items in the collection. There's a
lovely, calm "Portrait of a Woman" by Raphael—smooth-
featured, warm-skinned, grave-eyed—that is worth mention-
ing, though, as well as a suavely Venetian "Madonna and
Child" by Giovanni Bellini, and a small but completely
beautiful six-panelled "Profanation of the Host" by Paolo
Uccello. Piero della Francesca has a "Madonna," cool in
color and almost Flemish in its simplicity, but the high point

of the collection—an all-time high, in a sense—is his "Flagellation of Christ."

Piero, for all his limpidity of color and rectitude of design, could be enigmatic; and this painting, which, divided sharply down the middle, shows Christ being flagellated in the recesses of a courtyard, on one side, and, on the other, three personages—one a nobleman, another a priest and the third apparently an Oriental dignitary—all unconcernedly talking, has baffled experts to this day. I have no intention of attempting another explanation here, and I prefer to hasten on to add one more item to my list of the Museum's collection. This is a bas-relief, in profile, of Duke Federico's wife, Battista Sforza, and I'm sorry to say that—my notes being what they are—I can't now identify the author.

I know the subject, from another portrait of the lady, a painting of her by Piero, also done in profile, and very "like," as they say, in lineaments. In this instance, though, Piero was outdone from first to last, for his portrait is "posed," respectfully and as it were dutifully, while the sculptured relief, despite the relative intractability of the medium, is all life and animation. Lips parted, hair blowing, lean-faced and eager, she has the scrubbed healthy look of an up-state wife out beagling. It made me feel that, for all the occasionally ugly connotations of her family's name, she must have made a cheerful companion for the energetic Duke, her husband.

Bus Stop

We stopped for a week in Assisi, and profited by it. But the stay was so much longer than what most tourists allow for the town that, as had already happened in Orvieto, in the end we almost achieved the status of residents. Situated almost exactly halfway between Rome and Florence, just off the ancient Via Tiberini, and about 180 kilometers, or one hundred-odd miles, from either city, Assisi is admirably placed to be the goal of the kind of one-day bus excursions (there in time for lunch and the guided tour, and back to the Grand Hotel or the Excelsior in time for dinner) that have lately become so popular in Italy. These are run—and on the whole admirably too—by Cook's, American Express and all manner of other agencies. The town's religious importance as the shrine of one of the most winning of the Catholic saints, Saint Francis of Assisi, draws other visitors too, and the resulting influx —during the season, at least—is so great that it has imposed a certain rhythmic quality of its own on the town's diurnal activities.

Buses of more distant origin—the kind that, starting from Paris or from Geneva, for example, take their passengers, en masse, on what amounts to an only slightly stream-lined, modern version of the traditional Grand Tour of Europe—make Assisi a way station too. These, being a bit more leisurely in their progress, ordinarily stop overnight—a boon to the hotel keepers, certainly (who, in Assisi as in most of the other hill towns, have already seen their summertime business cut at least in half by the one-day, centralized tours) but occasionally a bit disconcerting to their longer-staying guests—like, in this case, us.

There is the daily hullabaloo in the lobby, when you come in to find it piled with luggage—each day, *different* luggage —and the rest of the space pre-empted by the tourists and the tour managers, the latter sometimes badged and visor-capped and sometimes not, but always harried, and all competing with one another to get their room allocations or, if they are leaving, their accounts straightened out at the desk— while outside, in the hotel courtyard, the bus drivers are already idling their motors, getting ready to travel.

There was always, for me, a certain amount of mild curiosity about what manner of people our next contingent would be. One of the graces of Assisi is that it is not built to the tight, concentric specifications of most of the other hill towns. It sits instead on a shoulder of the much higher Mount Subiaco, a dome-shaped, heavily forested eminence which rises some two thousand feet higher just west of it, and from which it is cut off by the gorge of the Torrente Tescio; and its shape is long and roughly elliptical. Assisi, lying tawny-pink as a lazy lioness, stretched out on its spur of rock, sprawls a little; and though the uphill streets are steep enough (most, indeed, are more passageways than anything else: sometimes stepped, or roughly paved in a diamond pattern peculiar to the town, and deeply guttered against the rainfall, the majority of them are completely impassable for a motorcar) the main roads, running lengthwise of the slope, go up in a series of sinuous zigzags: from the plain to the town and then back and forth slantingly through the town to the Basilica, the famous double church of San Francesco, up from there to the Piazza del Commune, and then, loopingly still, to, eventually—but by then the street has become a path, overgrown with grass, through the fields—the ruins of the once mighty fortress, the Rocca Maggiore.

Our hotel, the Albergo Giotto, fronted on the via Fontebella, the zig (or zag) leading from the Basilica to the Piazza. We were quartered at the back (by choice, incidentally, for we'd early learned that the street noises at the front, what with motor scooters rocketing back and forth and trucks gunning their motors against the gradient, can be frightful in the early morning), and we were lucky in that the room opened on a balcony or terrace—or rather a section of one, for the terrace ran the length of the building, and was partitioned off by a series of low balustrades between rooms.

It was a wonderful place for breakfast, or indeed for lounging at any time, for the view was magnificent—down upon the tiered roofs below and then out across the broad Umbrian plain, sprayed with olive groves and checkered here and there with the denser green of tobacco fields, to the far hedge of hills, each with its walled and turreted town—Spello, Foligno, Trevi, Montefalco, and so on—rising to the south.

Outdoor life on the terrace gained a certain piquancy from the fact that we rarely knew from one day to another who our next-door neighbors would be. They were always different as the busloads came and went. They were also almost invariably friendly.

Home, I've observed, is a word whose meaning expands with distance. For our fellow countrymen it had grown in Assisi, like a telescopic view, until it embraced not only the home town or the home state but the whole home country, and they greeted us with a confident and also confiding friendliness they would never have accorded a stranger elsewhere; in the week that we were at the hotel I got, if not a cross-section, at least a quarter- or an eighth-section view of the tourist in Italy—not, like the art, *in situ*, but actively in transit.

Not all our terrace companions were traveling by bus, though the majority were, and for that matter all were not Americans. There was the Australian couple who turned up one day: he a short, wiry fellow somewhere along in his fifties, name of McKenzie, and she a plump, placid, gray-haired woman of about the same age. They were on their way around the world, heading westward, and they'd already done the Orient. Ahead of them lay France, England and the USA, as Mr. McKenzie called it, so Assisi was very much a way station for them. At home, he was a chicken farmer, he told us, and then paused a moment. "I'm a chicken farmer without a chicken to my name," he added.

His wife smiled indulgently, and suddenly, for me, there was an echo in the remark. Like the shot heard 'round the world, I could hear it reverberating in Hong Kong and Istanbul, in Calcutta, Cairo and Athens, as he'd used it to strike up a conversation with this or that stranger along the way.

It turned out they had sold their farm to make the trip— "Pretty place, too, just out of Sydney. But we just up and dumped it," he said, while his wife, in wifely fashion, slid in parenthetically from behind him, "Of course, the children think we're quite mad!"—and would probably buy another and start over when they got home.

"Well, Mum, if you're going to do a thing I say go ahead and do it," he tossed back to her in husbandly fashion, and then, to me: "And it's something we did always count on doing. Yes, sir," he went on. "I'm a chicken farmer without a chicken to my name."

"Earl and Beth, though," his wife repeated, "they think we must be out of our minds."

I admired them, as I also admired, though in differing fashions, the nurse from San Francisco who shared our terrace one day, and the two girls from Minneapolis, one of whom had won five thousand dollars in a contest of some sort and who had immediately taken off for a tour of Europe, buying a Peugeot two-seater on the way.

We met them in a restaurant (my researches were not all confined to the terrace), where they were struggling vainly with the menu. Neither one spoke more than a word or two of Italian, and in the course of the conversation it developed that they were both engaged to boys back home and were planning a double wedding in the fall. It appeared too that their fiancés had heartily approved of the European venture, and when I wondered at this the younger of the two, and the prize winner, looked at me a little sharply.

"Why wouldn't they?" she demanded. "After all, they were in Korea." And she added, in what seemed a new approach to the traditional bachelor fling before marriage, "They said we might as well get the thing out of our systems."

I admired the nurse chiefly for her endurance. She was a large, bland, imperturbable woman, head nurse in a psychiatric hospital; and, as I recall, she had left San Francisco just ten days before, or about the time we'd been puttering around Arezzo, and by a fairly tight system of scheduling had flown to New York and then to Paris in slightly more than twenty-four hours, spent a half-day in Paris and then on (three more hours) to Zurich, in time to join the tour she was now engaged on. After that, the pace had slowed a little. But the tour (fourteen days, twenty towns and cities) was only a time-filler anyway; when it ended, back in Zurich, her next destination was to be Vienna, where she was due to pick up a friend for another tour, this one through the Germanic countries.

It was Europe at a gulp, all right. But she wasn't even winded, and it goes almost without saying that she knew no French, Italian or German—why should she? Lack of language seems to be the least of the bus tourists' problems nowadays, and given the high degree of organization and the speed of travel their nonchalance about the matter is understandable.

Girls predominated on the tours, usually in pairs, though there was a surprising number of women traveling alone. (Single men were practically non-existent.) Next came married couples and families, and the ages, I noticed, advanced about a decade with each category. It was difficult for me to figure out just how much, or how little, any of them were getting out of the adventure.

There's no question that the tours are run with a truly commanding efficiency. They are cheap. (The two-week tours, for instance, generally cost around two hundred dollars, most meals and all lodgings included, and you can't do much better than that, no matter how wise you are in the ways of travel.) Their greatest value, it seems to me, is to women, particularly women traveling alone, who would otherwise be too daunted by the dangers, real or imaginary, that might confront them to venture into Italy at all.

The trouble is that it's sightseeing skeletonized; what is lost is the flesh and blood and savor of the country, while the speed of travel seems to breed a kind of urgency of its own. I still recall another lone woman—plump, blonde, a little brassy but cheerfully so—who was also an overnight neighbor of ours on the terrace. She came from Detroit, she told us, and she was on a tour which had already taken her to Venice, where they had stayed two days.

"Or just one too many for me," she added briskly, and I stared at her in amazement, too awestruck to ask why two days in Venice was too much for a person who had traveled over five thousand miles to get there.

Later, though, I pondered it. It may be, of course, that she really didn't *like* Venice. There are those who don't, including a number of Venetians. (The winters, they say, are awful.) On the other hand, it may be that something of the magic of

the city will sink in afterward; after all, she will have her snapshots, postcards and Venetian glass souvenirs as reminders.
And again, she would probably never have seen the city at all
if there hadn't been a bus tour to smooth the way for her.
But it did seem a long way to go for so little benefit.

As I've said, not all the tourists are Americans, and indeed
there appears to be a certain seasonal pattern about the na-
tional movements. In general, I was told, it's the Scandinavians who arrive first, hurrying south at the first sign of spring
to escape their northern winter. Then come the British
(though they tend traditionally to make Florence their headquarters), followed by, in sprinklings, the French and—by
that time, in full summer—the Germans and the Americans.
There is naturally a good deal of overlapping, but when we
were there, toward the end of July, it was the Germans and
Americans who, true to the schedule, predominated. There
were still a few British about, but the Scandinavians, apparently, had gone home en masse to enjoy their midnight
sun.

There was also a surprisingly large number of Italians. Not
unnaturally, the Italians do a good deal of touring about their
own country, though for the most part they do it, sensibly,
out of season. (In the summer they head, whenever possible,
for the seashore, crowding the beaches all the way up from
Naples to the border.) They are especially fond of Assisi,
however, and for deeper and more varied reasons than the
rest of us.

For Assisi is not only one of the most beautiful of all the
hill towns; as the sanctuary of two of the saints most be-
loved by the Italians—St. Francis of Assisi and Santa Chiara
or, as we call her, St. Clare—it is also a religious site of great
importance and hence a point of pilgrimage ever since the
Middle Ages.

There are interesting parallels between the two figures.

Both were born in Assisi, and were fairly close contemporaries. Francis, son of a well-to-do merchant named Pietro di Bernadone, was sixteen and something of a blade, apparently (his conversion came later), when Chiara was born, in 1198. Clare's family was prosperous, too. Both were friends, and both eventually dedicated themselves to poverty, largely as a protest against the worldliness of the Church at the time. Both founded religious orders—Francis, of course, the Friars Minor or Franciscans; she, the Order of Clarissa, or "Poor Clares."

Both are buried in Assisi. Their respective churches are at opposite ends of the town, and Francis' is by far the more imposing. The church of Santa Chiara sits in an almost rustic setting, with orchards around and below it, fronting on a large, ramblingly proportioned, quiet piazza; and its pent-roofed façade, banded transversely in an echo of the Pisan fashion, relieved only by one round-arched, smallish portal, a rose window above and, above that, a smaller, round skylight, is plain to the point of austerity.

There is, unfortunately, an air of the makeshift about the structure. The church was begun in 1257, only four years after Chiara died, and it was completed three years later, in 1260, so the style is still Romanesque in essence. In the century following, however, side chapels were built on, a little awkwardly; and still later a row of almost grotesquely ponderous buttresses were added—I'm sure unnecessarily, but the Gothic influence had by then grown more powerful in Italy— to sustain the not overly high-ceilinged nave. Later still, in fact only a half-century or so ago, the square-topped campanile was topped, also a bit incongruously, with a steeple.

The interior, with its raftered, Romanesque nave, is dim and a little bare. What frescoes there are are placed scatteredly and are not in the best condition. To be frank, the main interest of the church is for the antiquarian and the devout; a chapel in the right transept houses, among other relics, the most sacred "Cross of San Damiano," a large, crudely carved Crucifixion, in wood, painted and gilded, which according to the legend actually spoke to Francis as he was praying, commanding him to "go forth and rebuild My Church," while, in the crypt below the main altar, is the body of Santa Chiara herself, laid out in her black nun's costume, the face black and wizened too, under the white coif, in a brightly lit, glass-paned niche.

The church, then, with its companion church of San Francesco, is one of the points of pilgrimage in Assisi. Nuns are the most numerous, not only of the Clares but of other orders; they come in busloads, just like the more mundane tourists, and the buses champ at their posts in the piazza while their passengers, decorous in demeanor but bright-eyed and obviously excited by the excursion, go whispering about the interior. Groups of children come, too, from the convent schools.

But to me somehow more affecting were the pilgrims of still another category, the groups of village people who had come with their parish priests to visit the sacred sites. They had the marks of farm life all over them. The men were hard-handed and seamy-faced, and dressed in the heavy black worsted "best" suits that are the sign of the countryman all over Europe. The women were broad-hipped and solid, and except that they had come by motorbus and were dressed in different fashion they were probably the replicas of all the pilgrims who have been coming in bands to Assisi from the Middle Ages to the present—as were too, no doubt, their priests, usually young, angular, thin-cheeked, and tremendously alive to their responsibilities as shepherds of the flock.

I saw them in the churches and also on the streets of Assisi and—now, as I suppose, as always: like tourists everywhere—it was the men who tended to coagulate, shuffling along by twos and threes, looking footsore and self-conscious, while it was the wives who darted about, pricing, bargaining and oc-

casionally buying the souvenirs and other bric-a-brac set
temptingly out before the shops along the way.

San Francesco, as I've said, is immensely the more impressive of the two basilicas. Built on two levels—the Lower
Church jutting out pierlike over the slant of the hill below it,
and the upper one rearing above it—it is, if not the highest,
certainly one of the most massive religious structures in Italy.
It too is, and has been for centuries, a point of pilgrimage,
and by what seems a mixture of planning and happy accident
the whole complex, interlacing, rambling edifice, as it clam-
bers, so to speak, up the hill, is admirably fitted for that
purpose.

In a sense it is an inversion of the usual church plan, for
the Lower Church, the one whose entrance is most commonly
used, suffers more than most Romanesque churches from lack
of illumination. Low-ceilinged and mightily columned and
vaulted (as indeed it has to be, for its masonry supports the
whole weight of the second or upper church) it is, in atmosphere, though not in actuality, the crypt. Though the body of
St. Francis is interred in the real crypt, still lower down, the
feeling here still is cavernous. The decorations are rich indeed
—works by Cimabue, Giotto and a host of others, including a
lovely, oval-faced "Madonna" by Simone Martini—while even
the groins of the vaulting are painted, with an almost Byzantine richness, in intricate geometrical patterns. But one is
forced almost to grope one's way among them; and I was interested, and a trifle amused, to note that several of the monks
or friars who serve as guides used flashlights to point out the
features of the paintings they were talking about.

Lights twinkle, here and there, though, from the banks of
candles set before the innumerable small chapels let into the
side vaulting, and the stillness is relieved by an occasional
tinkling of little bells as a priest performs Mass or, almost as
often, celebrates a wedding. San Francesco is a seminary as

well as a church, and since every priest is required to perform
Mass at least once a day, the chapels must be in considerable
demand.

Assisi is also a great place for weddings, and a good many
of the participants used our hotel, the Giotto, as their headquarters, winding up with the bride being photographed in
her finery in the lobby, while long tables were being set in the
dining room for the banquet afterward.

The Upper Church, with its long tile-floored nave and high,
regularly cross-vaulted ceiling, seems, by contrast, all light and
clean geometry—its beauty resting on the simple harmony of
just, true proportion that characterizes Romanesque at its
best. The great treasure here is the series of twenty-eight
frescoes by Giotto and his school, detailing the story of San
Francesco from his early acts of generosity and pious dedica-
tion to the miracles which are believed to confirm his saint-
hood. They almost literally cover the walls, and there was for
a long time controversy about the paintings, particularly as
to how much of the work should be attributed to the master
himself and how much to various of his pupils. It seems
fairly well established that the greater part was done by the
pupils, with Giotto himself working with them, touching
up details here and there and in general acting as co-ordinator
and supervisor.

Such was the custom at the time, and in view of the relatively short time it took to complete the enormous undertaking—five years, or from 1305 to 1310—no other explanation seems plausible. The question that still torments the
specialists is: What parts are by Giotto's own hand, and what
by his followers or apprentices?

To my mind, it hardly matters, and I'm sure it mattered
even less to the artist's contemporaries. Such great cycles were
intended primarily as a sort of huge picture book for the pilgrims to pore over, and the impact on them in this case must

have been overwhelming, as they came up from the darkness and the Apocalyptic atmosphere below to the sunniness and serenity of the church above.

Perhaps because of this educative intention, the series as a whole is a bit matter-of-fact in its imagery. When Francis, for instance, "sustains" the Church, he does so physically, bracing himself against it as it totters, and the feeling throughout is less poetic and allusive than that of the series Giotto later did, on the life of Christ, for the Arena Chapel at Padua —to my mind far the greater work. But then the aim in the latter case was not so much to instruct the peasantry as to please a knightly, and supposedly more sophisticated, company, the Cavaliere Gaudenti, or Celebrant Knights, of Padua —and artists in Giotto's time, rather more than is the case now, had to consider the needs and demands of their audience.

The very simplicity of the treatment, however, gives the Assisi cycle charm, and—Giotto being Giotto: who was it said that he "loosened the tongue of art"?—the whole concept is marvelous in its mingling of naturalistic narrative fluency and poignant emotion.

There are little ironies, and even a few mysteries, for the outsider at least, about Assisi and the legend of Saint Francis. It is odd, for instance, that the saint who preached poverty and self-abnegation above all else—who, in fact, was violently opposed to any show of ostentation in churchly or any other affairs, and who made his headquarters in a half-ruined chapel, the famous "little hovel," in a small plot of land, or porziuncula, in the woods outside the town—should be enshrined in one of the most sumptuous churches of all Christendom.

It is worth noting too—as has been pointed out by others, notably Eugenio Battista, one of the closest contemporary students of Giotto and his paintings—that the scenes in the fresco cycle in the Upper Church, depicting the saint's career and planned certainly under official supervision, tend to underemphasize this almost fanatic insistence on poverty of his, and to stress instead his miracles and his importance as an arm, an emissary, of the Pope.

There is an even greater irony in the circumstances surrounding Francis' death. He died, aged forty-five, on October 3, 1226, in the chapel in the porziuncula, and probably of malnutrition, having practically starved himself to death— died singing too, according to the accounts, for he not only must have been in an exalted state but had all his life urged his followers to be "joyous" in celebrating their faith—and upon his death his body was taken by a group of his disciples, headed by his close associates, Brother Elia and Brother Leone, to the little church of San Giorgio and interred there.

Only two years later—an amazingly short time in view of the traditionally slow, cautious movement of the Church in such matters; but Francis' fame and the veneration felt for him were already enormous—he was canonized, and the day after that, on July 17, 1228, the construction of the present Basilica was begun, the cornerstone being laid by the Pope, Gregory IX, himself. It was well enough under way two years later for the body to be moved to it. But meantime the whole plan had met with determined opposition by a considerable faction within the Franciscans themselves. This was led by Brother Leone, who inclined to take seriously the saint's interdictions against just such magnificence as the new church would embody. Though this group lost out in the end, and the building of the great edifice—pushed on by Leone's former comrade, Brother Elia—continued, feeling ran so high that when the transfer of the body was made, on May 25, 1230, it was done at night, as secretly as possible and with an armed guard along the way, for fear the Leone faction might try to wrest away the remains.

The move was engineered by the same Brother Elia, who has been described as "a courageous and authoritarian man" —and apparently was—and to avoid further conflict, possibly within the church itself, it was thought best to seal the body secretly in one of the walls, instead of placing it openly in a proper crypt. This, again, was done with such thorough secrecy that when the time came—many years later, and after passions had died down—to make the final transfer to the crypt, there was considerable difficulty in locating the remains.

All this occurred in the thirteenth century, when violence was commoner than now, when church towers were built to do double duty as fortresses and bishops led armies, and the whole incident must be viewed in that light.

But it was also a period of increasing pomp and ostentation in some areas of the Church; and it occurs to me now that the cult of poverty, so sternly advanced not only by Francis but by so many other holy men and women of his time, was much more of a rebellion *within* the Church than is frequently realized—as the struggle over poor Francis' remains would indicate.

To return to the paintings, though, whoever directed the choice of subject, and whoever and however many of the artists of his atelier may have helped, Giotto's genius shines through, and there is a vitality about them that had never been seen in art before. The thirsty shepherd, for example, really *strains* toward the spring that Francis had miraculously opened in the rocks for him; Francis is believably sturdy as he upholds the tottering church; and there is infinite drama in the quick, restraining hand that a friend lays on Francis' angry father's arm, ready to strike, as the young man, beginning his career of abnegation, divests himself publicly of all his finery in the streets of Assisi.

Otherwise, quite simply, the charm of Assisi is the town itself. As I've already said, it's unlike the majority of the hill towns in that it sprawls a little; and this, coupled with the warmth of the incomparable pink Subiaco stone of which its buildings are constructed, gives it an ease, a quality of unconstrictedness that most of its sister towns lack. To be sure, it has its peculiarities, and the ones that follow I have listed only at random.

It is famous for its swallows—the big ones called rondine, hardier and more raucous than our American variety—which are constantly in the skies, swooping and circling around the church towers and indeed often diving boldly at us on our hotel terrace.

The house windows are heavily barred, hinting at a warlike past; and in fact Assisi's past *was* warlike: it was for centuries engaged in usually senseless conflict with its neighbor Perugia, and Saint Francis himself, in his wastrel youth, was captured and held prisoner for a year after one of the battles. But the house walls around the windows now are festooned with flowers. (Even in Italy, where geraniums grow like trees and lilies swell to the size of shrubs, Assisi is notable for its flowers.)

It is famous too for its porti dei morti or "dead men's doors." These are narrow apertures beside the main portals of the houses and are another peculiarity of the town. According to one legend they were used as a defensible entrance, or escape route, for the occupant against streetfighting; according to another, they served as a passageway kept inviolate until the time came for a burial. In any case, they are now walled up, permanently and peaceably, whatever their original purpose.

The huge, round-towered fortress and the grassy grounds around it are now a favorite resort for picnickers, most especially the pilgrim villagers. The pilgrims are not rich, and they are country people to begin with; eschewing the restaurants, they bring their lunches in baskets, along with their wine, and it's seldom indeed that one makes one's way up to the Rocca without coming upon a party of them, the men unbuttoned and the women relaxed, clustered cheerfully eating and drinking in the shade of one of the ancient towers.

It's a lazy town, too. Where Arezzo is noisy and Lucca businesslike, Padua bustling, Assisi's pace is slower. Friday and Saturday are the market days, and then half the Piazza Communale is roofed over with tented stands and—a typical Assisan touch—asoar with tinted, tethered toy balloons. Other days the piazza is calm and more or less empty, with a minimum of the congregating, arguing and gesticulating that is common, day-long, in most of the other towns. The whole atmosphere is peaceable; even the tides of tourists don't affect it much, and though the shops along the zigs and zags of the main street have their wares set out temptingly (highly glazed ceramics, along with wrought-iron ware, are among the local specialties)—and though too the waiters of all restaurants on the same route are out at noontime, snapping their napkins and barking at the newcomers—neither they nor the shopkeepers work hard at it.

Noontime is the busiest time, for it is then that the daily buses arrive and the overnight buses are leaving. After that, the town subsides. I recall one episode that to me epitomized the whole process. I was sitting in a restaurant at one of the U-turns in the loops leading up to the Basilica. There was a bric-a-brac shop across from the restaurant, and the street at that point was narrow. It had rained throughout most of the morning, which had made the tourists' lives miserable; instead of sauntering, they had found what shelter they could in doorways or in caffès and had clustered there, awaiting the time of departure.

Now, however, one of the departing buses was in difficulties. The turn, at best, required a certain amount of backing and filling, but now the slipperiness of the pavement added a hazard. The pavement slanted, too, in what must have seemed to the driver unpredictable directions; when the wheels spun, as they occasionally did, the whole enormous vehicle—Pullmans, the Italians call them, as I believe I have said before, and this one certainly looked as big as a railway car, in the narrow street—would slide a little, this way or that: *this* way, towards the restaurant and its array of tables, *that* way towards the étalage of the shop across the way.

It was a ticklish situation. But the Italians, all opinion to the contrary, are excellent drivers, and by a process of patient, skillful jockeying this one eventually got himself straightened out and away. What interested me, though, was the attitude of the passengers.

I saw only the row of those at the windows nearest me, and throughout the maneuver they had all been leaning forward and peering out, almost comically in unison, helpless to intervene but still doing their best to give body English to the bus in its backing and filling. When at last it got away they leaned back, again in unison, and the last sight I had of them they were, visibly sighing with relief, settling themselves for—what was it now, the next stop? Perugia? Or have we already been there? Spoleto? Trevi?

In the restaurant—it was called the Monaco, and by that time I was a familiar: the waiters had long since stopped flapping their napkins at me as I passed and Bruno, the barman, the only man I have actually known who could sleep standing up, was a particular friend of mine—in the restaurant we all sighed and leaned back, too. The whole town could relax for another day.

The Hill Towns Again

Sometimes I think that simple leisure was the keynote of it all. As I've said before, one of the reasons—the main reason, really—behind this last trip of mine to Italy was to see something more of the smaller towns and villages in the hill country of Italia Centrale, north of Rome. Every time I had been in the same regions before my attention, for one reason or another, had been focused on the larger centers; the lesser ones, for the most part, had been places that I looked back at for one brief, usually wistful glance, as I went hurrying past on my way to—where? Rome? Florence? Pisa? Verona?

I still remember one day, some years ago, when I kept noticing rows of small caverns lining the low sandstone cliffs along the road around Sutri, on the way from Vetralla, north of Rome. They weren't cliffs, actually, in the first place; it was rather that the ancient road, the Via Cassia, had worn its way down twenty feet or so into the earth and the soft rock it was built on, and the cave openings were too symmetrical in shape and too neatly grouped to be the products of nature. Some had had rough batten doors built on at one time or another, apparently so they could be used for storage, but most were open. All were abandoned now, moss-grown and overhung with vegetation, and occasionally there was a bit of decorative carving, worn wax-soft with age, around the entrances: we were past and well on our way to wherever we were going before I realized, with a feeling of awe that may have been a bit naïve but was real enough at the moment (and still is, to be honest about it), that what I'd been looking at was a row of Etruscan tombs—twenty feet or so away in space but considerably more than that number of centuries away in time—and yet so little thought of in the welter of still richer treasures around them that they went simply disregarded.

This time, passing the same way, we stopped and got out to have a look around. Three children on bicycles stopped too, I remember, and one of them, a little girl, called, *"Tombe Etrusche,"* and pointed. When we asked her how she knew she said that *"la maestra,"* their schoolteacher, had told them, which seemed to settle the matter. But they watched us curiously as we peered about, and in actual fact there was little to see there, in the dampness and dimness, except the dark yawn of sheer antiquity. This time, though, we did stop.

This time, then, I'd determined to concentrate on the in-between, and when I went through the better-known towns and cities it was, so to speak, with eyes averted. Otherwise, I stuck fairly close to my plan. Apart from the trip down the Val d'Aosta—after all, you have to get into Italy somehow, and who could think of a more dramatic way of doing it?— I spent most of the time in Umbria and Tuscany, with some spilling-over into Emilia, the Abruzzi and the Marches. Geographically, this is limited territory—some five to six hundred square miles at best, or rather less than the area of Long Island. (Can I really be right about this? I have checked, and I think I am.)*

* Even more surprising is the fact that this small area, with the addi-

But in the course of the summer I was in and out of some forty towns in the area—some of them, to be sure, for no more than a lunch, a drink and a look around (a few hours at most); some for overnight or even longer stays, while even when we stayed at one place even longer, as at Assisi, Arezzo, Orvieto and so on, we made innumerable side excursions into the regions roundabout.

Though I spent a full summer at it, I still haven't exhausted the supply. In structure, the towns of central Italy are almost dismayingly similar. In the smaller villages, the whole town is no more than a cluster of houses and alleys around a church, a public square and a trattoria and shop or two, all hemmed in by a crumble of walls.

Grown a little, big enough to rank as a commune, or a municipality, the town will have two squares, one the Piazza del Popolo, or People's Square, where the Palazzo del Popolo (say, Town Hall) is located, and the other the Piazza Grande, del Duomo or, possibly, della Repubblica. The main street, ordinarily, runs somewhere between the two, and if not called the via Garibaldi it is almost certain to be called the via Cavour, Mazzini or—if renamed after the fall of Mussolini—Matteotti. (The Italians are incurably political, of course, and Mazzini and Cavour were among the architects of the Risorgimento in the mid-nineteenth century; Matteotti, a martyr under Mussolini. It must be remembered too that the Italians, beginning away back in Roman times with the

---

tion of Venice, was the birthplace and breeding place of practically all the artistic production of the Renaissance. Genoa and Milan, for all their wealth and power, produced almost nothing; south of Rome there was nothing either, and though Rome *drew* many artists to it, it too produced extremely few men of consequence. This fact is really enough to make one wonder about the ever mysterious tendency of the artistic impulse to localize itself—fertilizing the Netherlands in one century, France and Spain in others, and so on. Not to mention the way the great schools of literature flitted from England to France to Russia, and of music from Italy and France to Germany, in their various seasons.

more or less self-governing municipie, have had a struggling, inchoate and, despite interruptions, tenuously continuous acquaintance with the principles of democratic government for a far longer period than any other country. The small towns, particularly, are fiercely proud of the heritage. This may be one reason why Fascism, generally, met with least success in these areas.) Grown larger still, the churches, squares, streets proliferate, and so do the noise and the traffic.* One thing about the littler hill towns is that they are, for the most part, blissfully quiet.

But though the framework may be the same, they are amazingly different in atmosphere. Some of them, like little Coreglia, in the Garfagnano region north of Lucca, are bustling. Some, like Poppi, high above the Campaldino Plain east of Florence, or like Montefalco ("Hawk Hill," I suppose one might translate it) down south of Assisi, are, possibly because of their remoteness, self-contained in atmosphere and a little austere.

I remember Montefalco (apart from the Benozzo Gozzoli frescoes in the one-time Church of San Francesco, now the Museo Civico, which are certainly worth the visit) for its wide, warm, sparsely treed circular piazza; and for the large, bland and, as it turned out, extremely knowledgeable woman in housedress and apron who came plodding across the piazza to greet us as soon as we'd arrived and were parking the car.

She was, she told us, the custode of the museum. But she was more probably the wife of the custodian. Hill-town people, I've learned, eke out their living by a scattering of jobs; farmers, off-season, work in the brick works, and vice versa, and her husband may well have been putting in a three-hour stint at the post office, sorting mail. Anyway, it was she who showed us through the museum.

---

* The castle, at about this stage, moves away from the town to a site above and commanding it—another sign, perhaps, of the insecurity of the nobles in the face of the restlessness of their subjects.

Alviano—a clump, so to speak, of the poor Captain's prizes, set against the foundation wall of the castle, and crowned by a particularly handsome early Romanesque lion.

Alviano—the fountain in the piazza, and quite possibly another of the Captain's prizes.

Bomarzo—the temple or belvedere at the entrance to the Parco dei Mostri

Bomarzo—the head of one of the monsters

Poppi—the main hall and the stairway of the castle—patched up a bit at the top, but still fairly breathing of antiquity.

Todi? Gubbio? Where? Anyway, Ghibelline.

The Piazza del Popolo, Todi—here functioning partly as a movie set.

Viterbo—the fountain, and the graceful thirteenth-century arches of the terrace of the Popes' Palace.

The thing that impressed me, though, was the promptness with which she showed up. The Gozzolis—retailing the same legend of San Francesco that Giotto did, rather better, at Assisi—are about the only things to be seen at Montefalco; and Gozzoli, though honest, earthy, earnest and industrious, was hardly an inspired painter. (There is also, though, in the museum a handsome, curiously stylized "Three Saints," by Antoniezza Romano.) In consequence, Montefalco, even at the height of the tourist season, is little visited. There the lady was, though, waiting for us, the moment we appeared— and the whole thing seems to me a testimony to the timelessness of the hill towns.

I remember she stopped in to get a key at her house, across the piazza, and called in to a neighbor next door to say something about watching a roast, before leading the way down the side street to the bare, brick-fronted museum-church. It was midday, siesta time; all the rest of Montefalco was sleeping. But she had been awake, and watching.

Poppi I remember as one of the really high towns, a real eyrie, like San Marino, San Gimignano and so on; and again the feeling I have about it is of a certain remoteness, a withdrawal: the main feature, the castle; and the main feature of the castle, the great, stately, staired entrance hall, now partitioned off partly into apartments and partly into offices for the town administration, but with its walls still studded with the carved blazons and crests of the long line of Medicean and other chieftains who had inhabited it.

Other towns, like Monteriggione and to a certain extent its fairly near neighbor, Radicofani, both in the Siena area, are mere shells of the mighty fortresses they once were. Monteriggione, particularly, almost qualifies as a "ghost town." Formerly, it was a papal stronghold, so heavily fortified that, as I believe I've mentioned before, Dante used its ring of towers metaphorically to describe the giants looming over the central pit of hell, in the *Inferno*.

The towers are there, and the walls too, in fairly good shape, and it was the sight of them that drew us up from the road as we were passing below. Inside, though, there is almost literally nothing: a few houses, backed up as if apprehensively against the inner side of the walls; a small brick-fronted chapel; a tiny drogheria or grocery store, which also doubled as a wine shop; a garage where, when we were there, two young men in Levis were working desultorily on an elderly farm truck—all fronting on a wide, bare, dusty clearing, as big, blank and bleak as a paradeground.

Radicofani, a quiet farm town now, is a bit busier, but it too is dominated by the sprawling remains of the castle, called the Fortezza di Ghino di Tacco, reaching down its walls to enclose the town and culminating in a truly gigantic tower or keep—so high, so commandingly placed that it overlooks all approaches, from Siena to the north and down almost to Rome in the south. Radicofani's stone is volcanic and gray, which gives the place a martial look; and as a matter of fact its past was grim and warlike indeed—as I learned when, prowling about the ruins of the fortress, I made the acquaintance of the young man named Mario Rappuoli, who is in charge of a weather station installed at the top of the tower.

Mario must be in his early thirties, slim, alert, pleasant-faced and, for all his minimal education, extremely intelligent and well-read. Except in the war, when he was captured in Africa by the British and set himself to learn English while a prisoner, he has rarely been farther away from his town than Rome. But he's a poet in his spare time—and not a bad one, either—and a prodigious reader; we have been in correspondence ever since, and he was good enough to send me a digest of the town's history, as it revolves around the castle.

It is too long and involved to go into in detail here, but it

is clear from it that Radicofani, in the past, has had its vicis-
situdes. It was always, apparently, a warrior's refuge of some
sort. A defensible site is a defensible site, and there are remains of primitive fortifications at Radicofani that go back
beyond the Etruscans. The main structure, however, dates
from 1154, when the newly elected Pope Adrian IV* ordered it
fortified.

The castle was completed four years later, and taken over
by Barbarossa himself after a few years. Barbarossa enlarged
it, but a century or so afterward, when it had become a focal
point in the Guelph and Ghibelline struggles, it was razed
completely by the Sienese. Rebuilt again by another Pope,
Boniface VIII, and again damaged in fighting, it passed in
1279 to the almost legendary condottiere, Ghino di Tacco
(who again rebuilt it), and when Ghino was assassinated a
few decades later it passed again to the Medici.

After that, except for some damage in a mysterious gunpowder plot in the early 1700's and some shelling during the
last war, its career has been relatively peaceful. Its present
half-ruined state is as much due to age as to anything else.
Otherwise, its early history was one of constant building,
shattering and rebuilding; and the fields on the plain directly
below the town are still littered with great jumbled areas of
rotted gray stone, the débris of all the past razings.

I read somewhere that the location of many of the cathedrals was determined partly by the availability of stone
nearby; and certainly the task of transporting the tons upon
tons of stone from the quarries to the building site, over the
primitive roads and by horse- or oxen-drawn wains and wagons, must have been a major factor in the construction. One
can't help feeling that the hill towns must have been faced

* The so-called "English Pope," born Nicholas Breakspear, whom the
Romans mistrusted and the German Emperor, Barbarossa, cheated, and
who was in so much trouble throughout his brief career in the Papacy
(1154-59) that one sometimes feels he could hardly have drawn a
safe, secure breath all the while he was in Italy.

with a similar problem, that of getting their stone all the
way up, up, up to their particular eyries.

And when warfare intervened—well, at Radicofani, as at
other fortified hill towns, I found myself wondering how the
townsfolk managed to get their crops in, in the midst of all
this wholesale, hearty destruction.

There are times, too, in the hill towns—and these are
among those one remembers longest—when the whole atmosphere is one of peace, serenity, benignity. You drop into
a town on impulse, as we sometimes did, and park the car.
You nod here and there and exchange a "Buon' giorno"
with the black-coated, broad-hatted elderly men standing or sitting under the plane trees in the piazza, watching discreetly;
walk about a bit, up one narrow, stone-paved, deep-shadowed
lane and down another between the barred-windowed, sagging
houses; exchange another nod or two or a greeting with
a group of children standing shyly in a doorway or with a
woman filling a big brass ewer at the pump in a piazza; peer
into the church and the courtyard of the castle; relapse at
last (and by now the town has accepted you; no one even
bothers to keep track of your wanderings any more) at a
caffè table under the trees in the same piazza centrale. . . .
Suddenly, the town seizes you, and you feel you could stay
there forever, dreaming away the days, the weeks, the years,
in this timeless haven of peace and benevolence.

The feeling is fallacious, of course. Life is hard in the hill
towns, money is scant and comforts minimal. The winters,
particularly, are stern. "E morta, morta qui, all' inverno," a
waiter told me in Montefalco, striking his head as he did so;
and the isolation all the year 'round is something you either
like or you don't like. Most hill people like it, being a little
ingrown by nature. Even so, my friend from Radicofani, Mario
Rappuoli, told me that television had been the salvation of
the hill towns.

We were sitting in the bar of the little locanda (read, "lodging") called La Rocca, the one caffè in the upper town: it was evening, and there were four men playing cards in a corner and a scattering of others at the bar; the rest of the place was jammed with men, women and children—whole families, in short—sitting sometimes over a carefully nursed glass of Campari, sometimes over a half-melted dish of ice cream or some other sort of gelati.

No one pressed them to drink up, or to reorder; in fact, the waiter, who was also the proprietor's son, a boy of about fifteen named Angelino—again, anyway, young—was so intent on the screen himself (where, a bit improbably, a Japanese movie with Italian voices dubbed in, was being shown) that it was difficult to get his attention when we felt like having another vino nero; and I saw the same scene repeated many times over, evenings, in other hill towns. It's a kind of public service the caffès offer, pretty much free of charge, to their fellow townspeople.

"Television—" Mario said. We had got to be friends enough by then so that he was bringing out carefully typed copies of his poems to show us: like the father with snapshots of his youngsters in his wallet, Mario "just happened to have them along," folded in a notebook he was carrying. But even he was giving the screen a good part of his attention. "Television," he told us, "has opened the world to us hill people."

Alviano was one of the timeless towns. The town overlooks the Tiber, in the hill country south of Orvieto, and we turned into it too more or less on impulse. We were looking for another village, called Bomarzo, and were not sure of the way, and we were lucky enough in Alviano to stumble on a man who was not only able to direct us but also told us a good deal about the background of Alviano.

This one was a ruddy, round-faced, cheerful, confident agent of the Ministry of Public Works, and he had an office in what had probably once been the guard room in the gateway of the castle. (The hall, beyond, had been converted into a cinema: showings, Thursdays and Saturdays.) And he knew the region, as a part of his job.

He set us right about the way to get to Bomarzo. It was only a short way off, in fact, though the route was, as usual, circuitous, and Bomarzo turned out to be well worth the visit. This was not so much for the town, though that too had a gaunt look about it, steep-streeted and rather craggy, which was impressive, but rather for the almost unique pleasure garden—now called the Parco dei Mostri or, roughly, the Park of the Monsters—filling, in a cascade of half-ruined, eroded statuary, now weed-grown, the valley below.

The garden, or park, was designed by Giacomo da Vignola, a fashionable sixteenth-century architect who specialized in country villas and their landscaping; and it was built for the Orsini family, according to a legend I haven't been able to substantiate, by a contingent of Turkish prisoners of war, taken captive and barracked there after the great naval battle of Lepanto.

There is a mystery here, as there is about most matters of legend. The battle of Lepanto occurred on October 7, 1571, and this fits pretty well with Vignola's dates. Though it ended as a victory for the Turks, a great many prisoners were taken on both sides. The Orsini forces supported the Venetians in the engagement.

The work, however—most of it of heroic size and carved en bloc out of the solid granite of the hillside—is clearly of expert manufacture. Far from being the product of simple seamen impressed as stonecutters, it was obviously done by experts at the craft, and it is hard to see (1) how so many trained stone-carvers, if not actually sculptors, happened to be serving in the Turkish Navy at the time, and (2) how they happened to be captured and transported en masse to Bomarzo.

It is possible, of course. I'm reminded of a passage I came across recently in a book about ancient Thailand, in which it was said that the arts were so highly prized that one of the main purposes of waging war, among the various chieftains, was the capture of skilled artisans to decorate the palaces and temples; the Romans, in their heyday, raided the Greeks for much the same purpose. And certainly the Bomarzan work shows a mixture of Western and Oriental influences—as if Vignola's Baroque ideas had been subtly suffused with Eastern imagery—that tends to support the legend.

The garden itself is on three or four levels, rambling down a kind of swale in the hill just outside the town; and proceeding from a small, round-domed, porticoed Grecian temple at the top, past a statue of a three-headed dog which serves as Cerberus to the entrance of the garden proper, to—eventually —a huge, stone, fountain-fed pool in the midst of a formal court, now, of course, rank with weeds and heavily eroded.

Scattered in between are such features as a pair of remarkably full-breasted, moon-bellied mermaids (the East-West mixture, again), one bat-winged and the other two-tailed; a really fine group of a lion and lioness attacking a dragon trying to make off with their cub; a huge figure of a man apparently engaged in rending a screaming woman apart; and a sizable stone banquet chamber, fitted with a long stone table and flanking benches, all hewn from the solid rock, which one enters through the yawning mouth of a lion.

There is also a massive figure of an elephant, bearing on its back a Ghibelline-battlemented howdah, and clutching in its trunk a writhing male figure, clad in the armor of a Roman centurion. East and West, it would seem, could hardly meet on more uncertain terms than these.

I noted a legend carved in the rock facing the pool at the foot of the garden, which says, as I recall, "Lascie ogni pensieri neri in quest' acque" ("Drown all dark thoughts in these waters") and the whole place was clearly meant for elegant diversion. There is a savagery about the fantasy, though, which is somehow made more disturbing by the uneasy blending of motifs and imagery, and it was hard for me to picture a company of merry-making guests of the Orsini, even in the days of the Renaissance, remaining merry for long in such surroundings. Yet, one must remember, people used to get a thrill—and maybe still do—out of the Grand Guignol, the Eden Musée, and the old-fashioned papier-mâché horror scenes one used to be whisked past on the scenic railways in the amusement parks.

I fell in love with Alviano, however, at first sight, and what I learned of its past, from our knowledgeable Public Works agent, only served to endear it to me further. The town itself is a more than usually compact little village: no more than a wedge of houses, really, set on top of a similarly wedge-shaped eminence overlooking the Tiber and its valley below. There is a small but exceedingly staunch-looking round-towered, dry-moated castle at the apex of the wedge, with a small, treed piazza before it; and the rest of the town consists almost entirely of a long, narrow, cobblestoned street, angling along the three sides of the wedge; a few still narrower side alleys crisscrossing it; and, in culmination, a long, low-walled *luogo*, or view, overlooking the fields, mostly planted in tobacco, sloping down to the valley below.

The main square is called the Piazza Bartolomeo d'Alviano; there is also, at the *angolo* of the street leading down from it, an asilo infantile, or nursery school, modern in construction and named the Principe Doria; and the tobacco fields are laid out in narrow strips, in a fashion that puzzled me obscurely, since it seemed unusual in Italy. The story our informant told us cleared up all these details. It provided, too, an odd linkage with Bomarzo.

For the piazza had been named after a sixteenth-century captain in the Venetian forces, who had taken over the town at the height of his career, had rebuilt and refortified it and had planned, eventually, to settle down ungreaved and with his sword put aside, as many another captain, from Du Guesclin on, had hoped to do before him.

The ornaments we had noted roundabout were all the fruits of his conquest. There was an especially fine, snarling stone lion which he had apparently had carted there, and which served as the guardian of the fountain in the piazza, and the walls of the great, round keep were studded with other trophies, in the way of lesser carvings and decorations, let into the brick work there.

As it turned out, however, poor Captain d'Alviano had little time to enjoy his prize. Venice itself was hard-pressed then; there were more engagements, culminating—for him at least —in the battle of Lepanto.

He was killed there. The town passed to his brother, an abbot, who, being more ascetic than most of his fellows in that era, had no use for it; and it fell, eventually, to the Dorias —the great seafaring Genoese family who at one time owned a good fifth of Italy—and the reason the nursery was named as it was was in commemoration of the fact that Prince Andrea Doria, who died only a few years ago, had on his death bequeathed the village and the land around to—well, to itself, or to the families inhabiting it.

Here we enter on one of the most obscure facets of life in the rural areas of Italy today, and for my interpretation I lean mainly on that of an Italian friend, a principessa herself, but now landless, who was a bit hard put herself to explain the ramifications of the matter.

The situation seems to rest, though, mainly on the fact that in Italy long-established tradition is stronger than current law. Since Italy is a republic, the Dorias didn't really *own* Alviano any more, in the feudal sense that they could collect their tithings from the inhabitants and control the activities of the village. Except for rents, such revenues should go to the state, and the inhabitants, as freemen, were perfectly at liberty to run their lives as they wished.

But, on the other hand, the Alviani had *always* paid tithes to the Dorias, for generation upon generation, and in return had been advised on the planting and handling of their crops and the management of their own and the village's affairs; and according to the Public Works agent the feeling in the town, when the terms of the will were made known, was only partly that of liberation—there was also a sense of being cast adrift.

The Doria family kept them in mind, however, and it was they who encouraged the Alviani to go into tobacco. The reason, too, why the plantings are in strips is that, having no other way to divide the land among themselves, the townspeople fell back on the one the French farmers used in taking over their lands and villages after the Revolution. They simply divided the land according to its value and uses—good, bad, medium; farmland, pasture, orchard and so on—and then split each one up amongst themselves. There are many areas in France where the fields are sectioned off in this way to this day, and it was the resemblance of the slopes around Alviano to these that had puzzled me.

It was the atmosphere of the town, though, that enchanted me, making me want to stay on and on. I have described that mood a few pages back and there is no need of going into further details about it now. Basically, though, it seems to me that the mood arises from a sense of harmony. As with some of the landscape views one gets from the hill towns, there are times too when the whole pattern of life inside a town falls into a pattern of complete serenity and accord. Everything *fits*, somehow: the composition of light and shade on the grass or the stones of the piazza blending perfectly with the warm, worn faces of the houses fronting on it; the small sounds of the life going on behind the façades—a call, a laugh, the burr of a saw in a carpenter shop or the plock, plock,

plock of a hammer; a radio, not too loud—these breaking in on the silences at just the right intervals, and then the silence recurring; the figures moving here and there, moving with the slow, smooth propriety of figures in a dream—and all combining, almost magically, to give the visitor a feeling of utter and lasting rectitude.

Time stopped, one feels, when the town reached perfection, and it arrived at that stage generations ago. Now, if only one could enter into it, and remain there. . . .

A Long, Last Farewell

One of the charms of the hill towns of Italy is that one never knows what one is going to run into, in them. As I have said before, and may say again, for all their similarity of design, the life in them is incredibly various; odd things crop up everywhere, and it may have been only no more than was to be expected that we found ourselves at a motor-scooter carnival, or "gimkana," at Arezzo, and in the midst of a movie production at the town of Todi. Sometimes, too, even tinier incidents added their peculiar color to a place and helped make it memorable. There was the man who insisted on talking French to us at the garage outside Narni, for example. I'll remember him; and certainly the episode of the old lady in the tobacco shop did its share to illuminate my memories of Orvieto. Yet each one was small enough in itself—so small indeed that I hesitate to recount them all, for fear that I won't be able to convey the special flavor they had for me.

What impressed me about the man at Narni was not so much that he spoke French but that his whole discourse was about the Paris department stores. Narni is a smallish town, about sixty miles north of Rome on the Via Flaminia, stand-

ing tiptoe, so to speak, on the edge of a steep declivity overlooking the valley of the Nera River, and surmounted by a
small but ponderously walled, square-towered castle on the
summit above. Narni was a stronghold in pre-Etruscan times,
when the Umbrian tribes ruled the region, but its fortifications are largely in ruins now, for it was sacked by the combined armies of Charles V and Francis I in 1527, as they were
on their merry way upcountry after the sack of Rome, and
apparently never recovered from it.

It is reputed to have quite a good collection of paintings in
its Pinacoteca, which is lodged in the Palazzo Communale,
including one of the better Benozzo Gozzolis, an "Annunciation," and a Ghirlandajo "Coronation of the Virgin," both of
which I had seen in reproduction. I didn't see them *in situ*,
however, for we arrived just after the stroke of noon—which
meant that the churches and museums were closed and would
remain closed, inexorably, until three o'clock or even later,
and we hadn't the time or the patience to wait that long.

As a result—and apart from an excellent lunch at a restaurant called the Cestola, with a truly spectacular view overlooking the curve of the river valley below—I remember Narni
chiefly from a strolling look at its external aspects: the high-
arched, cavernous loggia of the Priory, now serving as a lava-
toio pubblico, or public wash-house, with an odd little bal-
conied pulpit let into the wall above; the bleak-fronted, brick
façade of the Palazzo Communale, opening on a low, heavy-
vaulted courtyard; the round-arched, weather-worn portals of
the fourteenth-century Church of San Francesco; and, of
course, the narrow, twisting streets and side streets—all dozing now in the siesta—leading this way and that between.

There was also a small, irregularly shaped open space, the
Piazza Garibaldi, where we had a coffee and grappa afterward, which somehow, with its fortunate, fortuitous architectural arrangement—an ancient gateway here, a towered
house beyond, a fourteenth-century fountain in the center and

facing it a pink-stuccoed, porticoed Renaissance building, now housing a branch of the Banca di Roma—had an almost theatrical air about it. Like the equally irregularly shaped Piazza Coli Romano, in Rome, which it somehow reminded me of, it had a little the air of a stage set—its architectural vagaries not the result of accident, but planned, for the sake of dramatic values.

Our French-speaking acquaintance was only an incident in all this, then. He popped up from nowhere, it seemed, as we had stopped for gas at a garage on the outskirts of the town. He was old, but spry, with a thin, shrewd face, and he was on his way down from the village on a Vespa motor scooter when he spotted us.

And our car was a Renault Dauphine, with a 75 on its plates that showed it to be Paris-licensed. . . . So, Americans or not—for we had to confess to our American origin—we must know Paris: was the Galeries Lafayette still there, and as brave with brass and glass and as filled with merchandise as ever? And the Louvre—not the museum, but the big store across from it, on the rue de Rivoli, wasn't it? What a place that was, and again jam-packed with practically everything!

But that was true of them all, wasn't it—the Samaritaine, and the Bazaar de l'Hôtel de Ville? A man could wander for days in any one of them, and not exhaust their resources. So he went on, and we listened in astonishment, while the garageman filled the tank, checked the oil and water and so on. He apparently knew the man.

"*Lascia. Lascia,*" he muttered occasionally. "Pipe down." But the man paid no attention. He had lived in Paris for a few years in the 1920's, when he was young. He had worked mainly in the Citröen automobile factory; he hadn't been back since, and I couldn't help remarking that under the circumstances his French, though a little rusty, was more than adequate.

This, however, hardly concerned him. "Et Le Bon Marché.

Vous connaissez Le Bon Marché? Rue de Sèvres?" he yelled after us as we started off. I wish now we hadn't got away so soon, for I'm still puzzling about him. It was a hot, dry day, late August by then, and the town was Narni. To the visitor, such places are all-of-a-piece, inviolable, a compilation of age and tranquility. Somewhere, though, in that framework, one has to fit in an old man, a native, who traveled abroad in his youth and came back with the strangest memories.

As a boy, when I lived in Colorado, I knew a man, old Pop Parry, as he was called—one of the settlers in the region—who was still fighting the Utes and the other mountain Indians, long after their menace had vanished; and in Assisi, as a writer myself, I was intrigued by the sound of a typewriter, clacking away behind a lighted window high up in the house across the way from our hotel. I mention these only because in each case they gave a feeling of depth to the town—as was true, again, of our encounter at Narni.

I shall try to be briefer—let's say brief, anyway—about the incident at Orvieto. There was a similar feeling of a gain in my depth of understanding, again not easily explainable, in this occurrence too. Here it was market day, and the big Piazza Communale was filled with makeshift booths, and alive with farm people and traveling tradesmen, the ones selling their produce and the others, miscellaneous merchandise: as I see it now the episode centers on the brown bony hand of an old farm woman, clutching a fistful of money.

She was in the tobacconist's, along with a half-dozen or so others of us, mostly women, and the tobacconist's was on the Piazza. She was no doubt the grandma or even the great-grandma of a family at one of the booths outside, and she'd been sent to lay in smoking supplies for the lot of them. But she was *really* old. She was old enough to be reverting to childhood, and like a child she recited the list of purchases— so many packages of this and that brand of cigarettes, so much smoking tobacco, and so on. Like a child, she'd been supplied with the proper amount of cash to pay for it all; and like a child she watched while the tobacconist made up the order.

When the order was filled, though, she just couldn't bring herself to part with the money to pay for it. As I've said, it had obviously all been figured out beforehand, and she had the money in her hand. But it came to a sizable amount, and when the moment came she just couldn't bring herself to part with it. Her hand tightened on the wadded assortment of notes and coins she had been supplied with; her lips tightened and her wizened little head went down in a childlike attitude of stubbornness. . . . For my part, the main thing that interested me was the consideration everyone showed for the old lady's attitude.

The tobacconist's was near our hotel, which was the chief reason I patronized it, for the man himself was rather a sour individual. The Italian government had just issued a silver five-hundred-lire coin, to replace the paper note then current, and this apparently had given rise to a certain amount of counterfeiting; I remember that he had installed a small, square billet of marble on his counter, and he bounced every coin of the issue on it with a kind of vicious energy, to test the ring. The women in the shop were all big-busted, broadbodied, burnt-faced women, black-clad—like the old lady, farm women all, come to market—and all in a hurry to get back to their booths so as not to lose customers. Orvieto, too, is notorious for being a hard-hearted, hard-shelled, practical town.

Yet it was odd to see how everyone rallied round the crotchety old creature, coaxing, cozening her. Look, they said; you ordered these things, your folks want them, they gave you the money. Listen, nonna vecchia, grandma, you know yourself, you can't get something for nothing. If you want it, you have to pay for it. . . . Slowly, in the end—the old woman's face still pinched tight with reluctance and distrust—the fingers opened, the bills and coins spilled out onto the counter. The transaction was completed.

The incident at Arezzo was more complicated. Arezzo, as I've said, is a jazzy town, noisy, bustling, its caffès loud with radio and juke-box music, its streets and piazze roaring with the exhausts of cars and motor scooters. Yet we were a little surprised, going up on our first Sunday to explore the ruins of the Rocca, to find the carved-stone blazon of the Medici arms, let into the wall above the long, barrel-vaulted entrance, surmounted by another—this one a round, metal-backed enamel affair, black and yellow, the insigne of the "Vespa Club d'Arezzo."

At the moment, I took it to be just another instance of the celebrated Italian irreverence for their own past. I was wrong, however, for I learned on discreet inquiry that the sign in this case was only a temporary intrusion, and it had been put there in connection with a "gimkana," or driving contest, to be held that afternoon at three o'clock, which was sponsored jointly by the said Club d'Arezzo and the Esso Oil Company, and in which contestants from towns as far away as Florence, Siena and Perugia were scheduled to compete.

It was to be held on a large, roughly circular, scatteredly grassed, dusty field inside the castle, and we ate a hasty lunch that day, I can tell you, so as not to miss the proceedings. But it turned out we needn't have bothered, for though we got back to the Rocca only a little after three it developed that to the Arezzans three o'clock meant, not the *start* of the races, but the beginning of the preparations for them.

The laying-out of the course had to be completed, for one thing. A gymkhana is a test of driving skill, and in accordance with this a tight figure-eight had been laid out, with an added diversionary circle in the middle and only the briefest section of straightaway to provide a roaring approach to the finish line. What must have been hundreds of empty pop bottles had been collected to mark the course, and when we arrived a half-dozen or so eager Vespa Club members were setting them out, in double line and about a yard apart, all around the circuit. But there was a brisk breeze blowing, which also raised dust, and the bottles kept toppling over, and this necessitated a good deal of scurrying about to set them upright again. A lean young man, in a blue-serge suit and gleaming white oxfords, probably the Club president and mounted on a Vespa, cruised about, supervising the proceedings.

There was also a good deal of other adjusting to be attended to. Here and there, obstacles had been set up along the course: a darts target, set off to one side, which the contestants were supposed to spear as they passed, was one, I remember, and a kind of teeter-totter had been set up farther on, consisting of a plank pivoted in the middle, which they had to ride up and then, after it had teetered, ride down again. And neither one of these had, till that moment, been adequately tested; now it turned out that the target had a tendency to fall off the frame it had been mounted on, and the plank shifted on its pivot at the first testing try.

So, a covey of Vespa Club members went roaring off importantly on their scooters to fetch rope, mauls and stakes to anchor things more securely. The young man in the blue-serge suit kept riding around and around, inspecting, supervising.

Meantime, chairs were being put out under a tree near the finish line for the judges. Vendors, too, were arriving, setting up little stands to sell soda pop, gelati, fritelle, or fried cakes, and other small delicacies. A new and—although he was casually dressed, in an open-throated shirt and wrinkled blue cotton trousers—obviously more important personage arrived. A large, pleasant-faced, placid man, he had a vaguely American look and I figured him to be the regional representative of Esso, or some such. But I never got near enough to find out.

By now—and by now it was going on four o'clock—a fair-sized sprinkling of spectators had arrived. These were of the heterogeneous sort that turns up anywhere at a free show on a Sunday: groups of soldiers on leave, a few young couples, families out for the afternoon stroll, children, strays of all sorts, buttressed by squadrons of Arezzan and other Vespa Club members, who arrived in phalanx, parked their scooters precisely, and remained more or less in formation throughout. The young man in the blue-serge suit still cruised diligently, keeping his scooter at about quarter-throttle so as not to overshoot the confines of the small area he was supervising, and dragging one white-shod foot negligently to keep his balance. With all the traveling back and forth, the dust began to be a problem.

All this took time. But it was a lazy, leisurely, sunny Sunday afternoon in Arezzo, and the crowd, no doubt conscious that the show was free anyway, was remarkably tolerant. Around four-thirty, however, it began to grow restive. Faint hoots and catcalls began to be heard; as if at a signal, another dignitary—this one clearly *the* dignitary—arrived. He was a bland, portly man, with a jowled, Roman-nosed face, and he had a retinue of three other men, only slightly less jowled and portly, and there was something vaguely political about him: was he the mayor, the podesta himself, or a delegate from that office?

I don't know, but like all true dignitaries everywhere—at championship prize fights, at first nights, at opening-of-the-season ball games—he had known the precise moment for arriving: or was the time, perhaps, accommodated to his convenience? At any rate, the "gimkana" started at once.

It turned out to be an anticlimax. The contestants all had to wear crash helmets, and they had a Le Mans start (toe a mark, and then, at the signal, run over to the scooter, get the engine going and be off). But the course stressed control so much that all efforts at speed had to be abandoned. The curves were so tight and the obstacles so numerous that the contestants' pace was reduced to a crawl; and though this probably was a fine object lesson to the youths of Arezzo—in whom I'd already detected a more than usual tendency toward loud exhausts and hot-rodding generally—it hardly made for a spirited showing.

The contest, I recall, was won by a red-coveralled Vespa Club man from Florence, who had only one arm. He alone socked his dart into the bull's eye of the target; he alone made the circuit without knocking over a single pop bottle, and teetered up and teetered down the plank without mishap. He alone was able to make much speed on the straightaway, and he got a good hand at the finish.

But the crowd had already begun drifting away by then, children, soldiers, lovers, families fragmenting off on their separate errands. The race was over and we were halfway down the hill into the town before an idea that had been lying tantalizingly in the nether regions of my mind came bubbling to the surface, and I realized suddenly where it was that we had been. Unquestionably, we had been in the ancient tilting yard of the castle, and the races we'd seen—and it gave them a certain fortuitous dignity—had been in a sense modern replicas of the knightly jousting that had gone on there, centuries before.

The incident at Todi, on the day I'm speaking of, was just plain confusing, although it was some time before I discovered what the trouble was. I had been at Todi a few times before. It is a Tiber-side town, about halfway between Orvieto and Perugia, which makes it a convenient noontime stop; and it has, also conveniently, a plain but very nice restaurant, the Umbria, with a marvelous view out over the valley below.

To my mind, Todi is almost the quintessence of the hill town—in fact, an extension of it in the extreme compactness of its structure and the complexity of its general layout. Where most hill towns are, so to speak, corseted by one set of walls and fortifications, Todi is hemmed in—or has been, at various eras—by a series of them.

As one starts down the main street, the via di Borgo Nuovo, from the Piazza del Popolo, walking past the high-stooped, flat-roofed Cattedrale, with its truncated campanile, one passes the remnants of not one but *three* concentric rings of fortifications; Etruscan, Roman and finally Medieval. Since the arrangement of the town itself still reflects the progressive system of growth, together with the compaction within the walls and finally the bursting of bonds which followed each expansion, the twistings and turnings of the streets, vie, vicoli, viali and so on, that resulted are almost beyond belief.

In my youth—and in fact, even now—there was an ever recurrent episode in the fiction of the South Seas that never failed to enchant me. In it, the sloop or the schooner was driving in through the breakers, all sails set, toward the seemingly unbroken line of cliffs that guarded the headland. On it went, till it seemed that instead of the captain a madman must be at the helm. But stay! Just as it looked as if the ship must break up inevitably on the rocky shore a break appeared in the cliff, a watery passageway, narrow but deep!

The ship luffed, or whatever it is that a ship does under such circumstances; a moment later, its headway diminishing, it was threading the tortuous passage—to drop anchor at last in the quiet waters of the hidden lagoon beyond. Native proas, usually filled with dusky beauties, were already pushing out from the palm-fringed shore, to greet the newcomers. . . .

I was reminded of this in my wanderings about Todi's side streets: there too one is constantly finding one's self in similar, if non-nautical situations. Time and time again, I would find myself heading into what was obviously a dead end, with a wall, or a fragment of wall—even, sometimes, a section of old fortifications that had itself been built on, making it look all the more formidable—implacably barring the way.

I soon learned not to turn back too hastily, however, for almost invariably there was a sidling passage of some sort— often not even burro-wide—to another street, equally tortuous, or perhaps to a worn flight of steps and then up to a tiny piazza and another network of streets above.

Todi, too, by reason of its isolation, is very much an all-of-a-piece town. From the bulky Palazzo del Popolo and the only slightly less commanding Palazzo dei Priori at the south to the Cattedrale at the northerly end of the piazza, all the buildings on the square date from somewhere between the thirteenth and early fifteenth centuries; and though this span may have seemed enormous at the time,* age, so to speak, has compacted it, and one of the main charms of the golden-stoned, spacious piazza—as of the whole town, for that matter—is its architectural unity.

Or it had seemed so on our previous visits. This trip, though, there was something disturbing about the place. There was a statue midway of the piazza that I didn't remember having seen there before. It was a figure of a marvelously jack-booted, frogged-uniformed, saber-brandishing man in hussar's uniform, which seemed somehow a little out of place in the general framework of things. There were posters on the house walls too, showing soldiers going strenuously over the top in defense of a place called Concordia, and there were placards and blazons here and there, all bearing the arms and green-and-yellow colors of the same Concordia.

There is a town named Concordia in northern Italy. I had never been there, but as far as I knew it wasn't engaged in any

---

* And no doubt it did. As a partial indication, although the two palazzi face each other catercorner in the piazza, one—the Palazzo del Popolo —bears Ghibelline crenelations and the other, Guelph. The latter commemorates the triumph, around the turn of the fourteenth century, of the papal party over the Chiaravalle, till then the ruling family of Todi. Such stony evidences of ancient enmities close at hand seem merely venerable now. But they probably meant more to the townsfolk of the period.

hostilities. My bewilderment deepened when I came upon a neat brass plaque beside a doorway farther on, signifying that this was the offices of the United States Consulate—"Hours 10 A.M.—1 P.M., Monday Through Friday."

When I told all this to Mike Boerner, an acquaintance of mine (and a very helpful one) at the American Embassy at Rome he looked at me in mingled surprise and asperity. "We don't have a consulate in Todi," he told me. And he added, "If we did, we would never allow them to keep lazy men's hours like that!"

And it's true, we don't have a consulate there—nor for that matter do the Russians, though they had their offices under a big hammer-and-sickle banner just across the piazza, hours 8-6 daily.

The fact was, as we discovered soon after, that we had wandered onto what amounted to a vast movie set. Peter Ustinov was there, with a troupe, filming "Romanoff and Juliet," and he had not only taken over the town but had touched it up here and there to fit in with the script's demands.

They were working afield that day, which explained the quiet on the piazza. But around four o'clock they began returning, some in costume, some not, in a mixture of jeeps, station wagons and Italian sports cars. By that time we were sitting at a caffè terrace on the piazza, and we watched—as did, discreetly, a considerable number of the Todiani—as they disembarked.

Peter Ustinov strolled past, surrounded by a retinue and followed by a crowd of local children; and (I tell you, it was just like Hollywood: she was less than ten feet away) I saw his co-star, Sandra Dee herself, with another girl, both in pony tails, Levis and fulsome sweaters, and in animated colloquy with a bulky little man in a Hawaiian-style shirt and wearing a swordfisherman's long-peaked cap.

"But why *can't* we go to Perugia tonight?" Miss Dee was saying. And when the man shook his head: "But it's only a half-hour or so. And we *want* to go to Perugia. Why *can't* we?"

The girls were underestimating the time a little. But it's not very far away, and if it had been I they were appealing to I'd not only have let them go to Perugia; I'd have gone with them myself. The man, however, was obdurate. There was some business about retakes or some such and the boss had said everyone must be on hand. It was the meagerer amenities of Todi for Miss Dee and her companion, and not Perugia's grander Brufani Palace or the Trasimeno, that night, anyway.

As I've said, it just goes to show that you never know what you're going to run into in a hill town.

This chapter seems to be developing into a kind of grab-bag affair, as disordered and disheveled as the contents of one's luggage becomes after a summer's traveling. I'm afraid it will have to remain so, too: I've so much in the way of random comments and observations I still want to stuff in.

There are the moments of revelation—or say simply awe—that come suddenly upon one, blindingly, and at the same time illuminatingly, unexpectedly along the way. I had one such at Ravenna, looking at the mosaics in the little, light-as-a-bubble tomb of Galla Placidia, mother of Valentian III and Regent of the Roman Empire, tucked away as if in afterthought at the rear of the church of San Vitale. Is the Taj Mahal more beautiful, more jewel-like in its precise, miniature perfection? Yet the Taj Mahal was one of the climactic creations of a whole civilization, while Galla's tomb was built in the middle of the fifth century, at a period we ordinarily think of as the beginning of the Dark Ages, for the Empress died in Rome in the year 450, and the mausoleum had been built at her express orders.

But then all the architecture bubbles in Ravenna, even San Vitale itself, with its great domed apse and drum-shaped side chapels; everywhere, too, there are mosaics, and I found myself thinking: how extraordinarily important an established art style is, and what a prop it is to the individual artist! And why, then, are the artists always knocking that prop out from under themselves?

For Laurence, a day or so before, as we were driving up from L'Aquila to Rimini on our way to Ravenna, had made one of those remarks of his that I took to be particularly "pregnant." He said, à propos of what I can't now remember: "The difference between science and art is that science can build on itself, and art can not."

And it's true, of course; wholly, irretrievably true!

For science, by a series of logical, consistent, cumulative developments, can progress from the principle of the kite to that of the airplane, from the discovery of the magnifying glass to the telescope and then on to the exploration of the universe, or from the invention of gunpowder to the production of the H-bomb—which is one reason why the world is in the fix it is in today. In art, though, as soon as a style has reached perfection, or even as it nears it, the artists themselves turn upon it, twist it inside out, upend it—and then start all over again in another direction.

It was not always so, of course, or at least in earlier times the changes in direction occurred at less frequent intervals; and I can't help wondering if it all isn't related to the time, toward the end of the Renaissance, when the worker in paints or in sculpture (or in mosaic) ceased to be an artisan and became an "artist," with all the mixture of advantages and disadvantages the change implies.

It was then that temperament came in, and individual expression superseded the group variety. One of the most impressive things about the Ravenna mosaics, for example, is the absolute authority of their expression, the unchanging, unchangeable assurance they have. They exist apart, in a world of their own, and one reason for their power over us, I think, lies in the fact that they are based on an at that time firmly established style.

No one knows who made them, and in all probability they were made—like the sculptures on the Gothic cathedrals —by teams of artist-craftsmen working together. It was a form of mass production, if you wish, and I speak neither for nor against it. Certainly, the principle of individual expression has superseded it, apparently forever; and when an attempt is made to revive the same sort of group expression, as in the modern mosaics that blight the face of Orvieto Cathedral or the latter-day examples at Saint Mark's in Venice, the results are deplorable.* It was the formalized style, the almost pictographic mode of emotional expression and delineation that sustained the older ones, and—again, without regret: simply with wonderment—one can't help thinking how happy the anonymous artists must have been in . . . well, in their anonymity.

I had another minor revelation in the Arena Chapel at Padua. The Arena, or as it is sometimes called, the Scrovegni Chapel, after the name of the Renaissance family who built it, is a simple little church, set down on the site of a Roman arena in a corner of what is now the Botanical Gardens, or Giardino Pubblico, halfway down the Corso del Popolo

---

* One reason for the decline in the art of the mosaic is, ironically, the outcome of that same old search for perfection. The artists of Ravenna had tesserae (as the tiny tiles the mosaics are composed of are called) of only about two hundred different colors and shadings of color to work with. Technological advances have since progressed to the point, so I'm told, that in a plant like the great Vatican workshop for mosaics, tiles of more than twenty-eight thousand gradations are available. This *reductio ad absurdum* came about because of the *scientifically* laudable attempt to make the art of mosaic just as flexible, just "as good as" the art of painting—overlooking the question of why, then, bother about making mosaics at all and certainly proving again that science and art rarely mix.

from the center of the city, and I was looking at the Giotto cycle of frescoes there—as one must, if one is in Padua.

Ours was a wandering trip throughout, and in the course of it I saw several of the great fresco cycles, from the Benozzo Gozzolis and Ghirlandajos at San Gimignano to the Carpaccios at Venice. But it wasn't until that day in Padua that a thought—which had no doubt been forming itself in my mind for some time—suddenly coalesced inside me. It is still a bit tenuous, as most momentary revelations are, and it's difficult to put simply. But the essential thing about it was my realization of how much the Renaissance artists, working separately in space and consecutively in time and yet in a sense together, had done to form, rationalize, dramatize and finally to glorify the whole body of Biblical legendry.

The Giottos, of course, are a combined development of the lives of Christ and the Virgin Mary—thirty-eight panels in all, with a huge Last Judgment thrown in—and the Christ story itself is the stuff of which high drama is made, from the humble and yet miraculous birth on to the intense climax of the Last Supper, followed by the Calvary, the Crucifixion and the Resurrection. But the artists, reacting to this latent dramatic essence and reinterpreting it according to their own fashions, gave it added vitality, order and substance.

In that sense, it seemed to me, they were like pianists, say, working separately over some piece of great music and by their assiduity, by the depth of their study, finding newer, richer tonal and thematic suggestions hidden in it—and expanding these, in the end, from a mere series of notes to an intricately interweaving, cumulative interplay of harmonies.

There is nothing especially novel in this idea. But this aspect of it was new to me, and in the narrow, bare, rectangular chapel at Padua it struck me with something of the force of a revelation. It came at Padua, I think, because Giotto himself is a culmination and a turning point, for in his work he not only liberated painting from the rigidities of Medieval and Romanesque styles but opened the way for all the developments of the Renaissance, and the Paduan frescoes are unquestionably one of his greatest achievements. I was interested to note, too, how the artists seem, almost unanimously, to have favored certain scenes and episodes of the legend for fullest development. It's no accident, it seems to me, that Leonardo's "Last Supper" is one of his climactic pictures; it is a high point in the Giottos too, as it is in many other similar instances. There is even a version of it (and an oddly unconventional one too, in which Christ and his disciples are seated at a round table) in the refectory at the Abbey Church at Pomposa—and the episode, along with the Crucifixion and the Resurrection, is among the ones which appear to have attracted them all most strongly.*

In the legend of Mary, it was the Annunciation, with all its implications of mystery, magic and femininity, that had the greatest appeal, and it was interesting to me to compare the variety of moods and emotional significance with which the different artists invested it. As I've said before, Fra Angelico, in the Museo Diocesano at Cortona, gives a feeling of breathlessness to the scene, and this feeling is heightened in Filippino Lippi's version in the Museo Civico at San Gimignano:

* I am speaking of the Renaissance artists now, who gave most of their attention to the tragic finale. Without having investigated the matter much, I have the impression that in later periods, such as the eighteenth and nineteenth centuries, attention shifted to less dramatic scenes, like the Sermon on the Mount and the Miracle of the Fishes (scenes which the earlier men tended to gloss over), and it occurs to me that it would be interesting if someone were to undertake a study of the changing tendencies in this respect, in their relation to the changes in religious and social attitudes, from one era to the next. With regard to the "Last Supper" particularly, was it the implications of greed, treachery, intrigue and betrayal, the smiling face and the stab in the back—all so much a part of the preoccupations of the Renaissance way of life—which attracted the artists of the period, and made this phase of the legend so vivid to them?

here the angel, settling to his knees in a subsiding swirl of draperies before the Virgin, seems to have rushed post-haste directly from Heaven to announce the coming miracle.

In the same town, in the Duomo, Ghirlandajo presents the angel almost as an intruder, reaching out hesitantly to interrupt the Virgin, who is shown kneeling at her devotions. Carpaccio, in the Ca'd'Oro, in Venice, adds deliberation: here the angel advances slowly and solemnly, while the Virgin, again at her prayers, lifts one hand gently, palm towards him, as if temporizing. Piero, realistic to the last, in his version in the Duomo at Arezzo, gives the episode a regal quality. Mary, nominated Queen of Heaven, is portrayed here in queenly guise too, and her attitude is almost one of hauteur as, standing, framed in the columns of a Grecian portico, she receives the messenger angel. God, looking down from above, points a finger as if to introduce His emissary.

This last, this final, final chapter is long and promises to get longer. I can't help it; there is so much still that I'd like to get into it. We talked again and again, en route, about Laurence's theory of the fatal discrepancy between the arts and the sciences, and its implications and its ramifications.

The Orthodox Jews, I believe, used to celebrate the New Year by throwing out all their china and cooking utensils and laying in a new set, as a symbolic gesture of cleansing and starting over; the artist—the modern artist, that is— more vehement in his rebirth, periodically demolishes the whole house and starts rebuilding. And one wonders: why? For one thing, he makes so much trouble for himself in the process.

As I've said earlier, it was not always so. In the journeyman days of the arts, all the painter strove for was what might be called a "readable" picture, one that told its story competently and quickly, and to accomplish this readily an established technique was almost an essential; artists then did

learn from and build upon the works of preceding generations.

It was Giotto who changed all this, and in his breaking-
away from the dominant Byzantine tradition he may truly
be said to have paved the way for all modern art. Yet for
centuries after him the ideal of a possible "perfection" lin-
gered, this time with the Greeks as the criterion; and from
Vasari on down to Ruskin it was felt that if the artists only
studied harder and harder, building on the achievements of
their predecessors as these had upon theirs, they might hope
sometime to arrive at the level of a Praxiteles or a Phidias.

It seems a sterile concept now, as sterile in essence as the
idea of that superlative, supernal "lost chord" in music—for
its end result would obviously only have been a "perfect"
copy of the original. It is only the art fakers who strive for
that now, and, to the discomfiture of the museums and the
collectors, occasionally succeed. Yet it's the reason Victorian
art students were put to drawing so much from casts instead of from the living figure; in a sense (and it was a final
absurdity) the Praxitelian ideal had superseded reality, and
—again, to repeat myself a little—it was not until the rise of
the concept of art as an individual expression, with the artist
striving to infuse his own "temperament" into the representa-
tion, that the idea of a set goal of universal perfection, both
attainable and understandable by all, was finally rejected.

But at what a cost to the artist! For, with no established
technique as a means of communication, both he and the
spectator are a little at a loss and frequently at odds at the
start, and one of his major problems is that of making his in-
novations comprehensible and acceptable to his audience.

"I don't know anything about art. But I know what I
like." That remark, so often quoted derisively, seems to me to
be one of the soundest statements that could be made. Who

does *know* anything about art, to come right down to it, either among the artists themselves or among the spectators?

Not I, at any rate. And how much better off we all are than those others—the expertisers and the art historians, the authorities on provenance, prices, periods and so on—who know *all* about art, in their special field at least, but haven't the faintest idea what they really like?

"You'll be sorry," the disgruntled child says; and so, it seems to me, does the ignored or misunderstood artist—a child too, in many ways, himself. How else explain the stubborn persistence with which, in the face of all discouragement, he keeps trying to inflict his own personality on a resistant world? Only children, so far removed from death, and artists, so bemused with it, can have the same innocent attitudes toward mortality.

"You'll be sorry after I'm dead and gone," they say. "Just you wait. You'll be sorry!"

Van Gogh, Cézanne, Correggio, Rembrandt, Gauguin, and how many others, echo them. But it is still one of the chanciest of gambles, for there have been a host of others who, trading too heavily on a non-existent genius, were never regretted at all.

Still pondering the whys and wherefores of the hill towns:

It occurs to me that one of their advantages, for their inhabitants, is their cleanliness. Anyone who has been stuck in a doorway halfway up the road to the Rocca in one of them, in the course of a summer thunderstorm, can understand why the streets are so speckless and spotless: top to bottom, they are sluiced clean almost daily by the rain.

But there is a kind of tidiness about them that goes beyond that. My wife was struck particularly by the fact that even in the tiniest of them there is at least one, and frequently two or three, hairdresser's establishments; and the

girls, coming out of even the most ancient alleys and tene-
ments for the evening promenade, are always—bare-armed,
short-skirted, slim-legged—impeccable.

Something, too, it seems to me, could be done about the
popularity of the various saints in different countries as meas-
ured by the number of churches named after them. St. Denis,
I'd say offhand, is not only the patron saint but also the
most favored one in France.

In Italy, one of the most popular is San Lorenzo: how
often, from Portovenere down to Orvieto and beyond, and
from the earliest times to the latest, did we come upon little
wall sculptures, depicting the saint roasting uncomplainingly
on his grill. (The one in Portovenere, incidentally, is a particularly fine example, for though it dates from around the
twelfth century and is accordingly primitive in execution,
the body has been twisted a little, corkscrew-fashion, from
the feet up to the head, to show him in the very act of turning, or being turned, on the grill.)

Along with San Lorenzo come San Michele, who slew
the dragon, and San Francesco and San Martino, the gentler
ones, though not necessarily in that order. Among the
women saints, I'd say, it is Santa Chiara and Santa Margherita who lead the way.

Or about the subject of buttressing, which I pursued all
the way from Lucca across to Ravenna's San Vitale, and
never once came upon a true flying buttress. Why? The
Italians certainly knew about this northern development.
There was enough interchange between countries for that.
Yet they never wholly trusted it, and one remembers even
that when Milan Cathedral was building, in the year 1400,
French master masons were summoned to pass on the safety
of the construction design. Was it simply, as Symonds sug-

gests in his *Renaissance in Italy*, because the Italians still clung to the Roman flat-roof tradition?

But then, why was it that the Romans, with all their skill at engineering, never built towers?

We spent a good deal of time, too, as we traveled about ourselves, working out a guide for the visiting motorist traveling in Italy. Here, again, there seem to be a number of misconceptions—among them the notion I mentioned earlier that the Italians are wild, reckless drivers and that motoring in Italy is an extremely hazardous undertaking. I have not found it so. The Italians drive fast, certainly, but the European cars, as by now everyone knows, are small, agile and wonderfully maneuverable; though I know the statistics don't back me up, in my own experience serious accidents are rare. We drove twice from Paris to Rome and back by fairly circuitous routes, a distance of about four thousand miles all told, plus another thousand miles or so on side trips, and in the course of it we saw, or passed the scene of, just three accidents, none of them serious. This, I'd judge, is roughly the equivalent of a round trip to Colorado from New York, and I doubt if one could make such a journey in this country without seeing the remains of half-a-dozen or more pile-ups.*

The Italians are aggressive, too. Every meeting at a crossroads is the signal for a duel, and one disconcerting thing about such encounters for the Anglo-Saxon is that the Italian looks you right in the eye as he makes his feint to move out in front of you. Out of shamefacedness, guilt, a feeling of

---

* Another misconception, in my view at least, is the idea that the Italians are poor mechanics. In my own experience, they are excellent ones, though I admit it is a bit disconcerting, at first, to find them doing most of their repair work on the street, outside a hole-in-the-wall garage. But then, in New York, we let people build skyscrapers in the street—piling I-beams on the sidewalk and massing concrete mixers, trucks, cranes and other apparatus on the pavement alongside.

politesse manquée or just plain chicken-heartedness, we tend to pretend the opposing car isn't there at such moments. We look the other way, and wait for the other fellow to blow his horn—whereupon we turn our heads with a start and the affronted exchange of "Why'n't you look where you're going?" "Haven't you got any eyes at all?" and so on, begins.

The Italian has no patience with such weaseling. He issues his defi openly and boldly, right at the outset: for me, there was always something unsettling to find myself confronted with a car inching out from a crossroad—jockeying, so to speak, for the advantage—with its haughty-eyed driver staring remorselessly at me all the while.

I usually gave in, of course. But I didn't feel too good about it.

There are areas, though, where the Italian is surprisingly courteous and considerate. I have had people follow me for miles to tell me that I had left my turn indicator on, that a luggage-carrier cover was loose or that a rear door wasn't closed securely. Coming into Rome from the north, down the Via Cassia, we stopped by the side of the road at the entrance to the city in order to check the route through to the Janiculum, where we were to stay. We had hardly pulled up before a man in another car stopped beside us, asked our difficulty, and not only directed us but led us part of the way to make sure we were properly started.

In the town of Città di Castello we had much the same experience, this time in delayed action. We were planning to spend the night there, and we stopped on the way in to ask a man sitting in front of a shop on a small piazza to direct us to the Albergo Tiferno, the hotel that the Michelin Guide recommended.

He told us, in detail. But, small as the town is, the windingness of its streets confused me, and to my dismay, after a series of twistings and turnings, I found myself passing the same piazza, the same shop and the same man again. I waved, and he waved and shouted something. But I thought I knew where my mistake had been; I'd turned left when I should have turned right, or something. I drove on.

When I passed him the third time, though, I was too embarrassed even to look at him. I pretended he wasn't there, and we were well started on our third trip around when there was a great shouting and gesticulating from the people along the way (after all, they must have been getting used to us, by that time) and a moment later a Vespa motor scooter roared up and overtook us, with the shopkeeper perched on the pillion seat behind the driver. Determined to get us settled, one way or another, he had commandeered a friend and his Vespa, abandoned his shop momentarily, and personally guided us to the hotel.

The Italians are considerate in other ways, too. The hill towns, with their narrow, sidewalkless streets are made for the leisurely passage of the horse cart and the donkey. Motorcars are an anachronism, and the motorists themselves have accepted the fact and adjusted themselves to it. I held up traffic for at least twenty minutes on the main street of Orvieto, the Corso Cavour, while I backed and filled, trying to wedge—perhaps "swedge" is the better word—my way off the Corso, itself barely wide enough for two cars to pass, into a side street so narrow that it was only by inches that it would accommodate one.

No one showed any great signs of impatience. They all just waited—and by that time it seemed to me that half the town was involved—shouting advice and encouragement. The Italians wait, too, uncomplainingly (and I was always surprised to see it, for these are the same drivers who brook no compromise on the highways) at all minor stoppages in the streets.

If a man stops his car, rolls his window down and pauses to say hello to a friend on foot, for instance, the cars trapped behind him wait patiently, with none of the horn-blowing that would occur in similar instances in America. Horn-blowing, for that matter, is strictly prohibited in all the Italian cities and towns; and, anyway, why protest? If a man runs across a passing acquaintance and wants to exchange a few words with him, how else, under the circumstances, is he to go about it? It is only after a decent time has elapsed that the snapping on and off of headlights and the revving up of motors—the Italian substitute for horn-blowing—begins in the cars lined up behind.

Pedestrians, of course—when one is not being one himself —are a menace everywhere, but they are more than usually so in Italy, where the laws themselves are rigged in their favor. As a result, a sort of involved, involuted conflict goes on between the two factions in the streets. Triangular in construction, it reminded me of the imbroglios of the Renaissance, where the Guelph and Ghibelline struggles were complicated by the (literally) intramural dissensions that went on between the Nere and Bianchi groups within the Ghibelline party.

In the modern version, the motorists (the Ghibellines, I suppose we must call them: relatively, the aristocrats) may joust with each other in true Black-White fashion at the crossroads. But elsewhere, and particularly in the towns—the Guelph or pedestrian strongholds—they must combine forces, for in the towns the Guelphs not only outnumber them; they outpower them.

Horn-blowing is forbidden, as I have said; and, deprived of his horn, what is the motorist to do to blast the plebeians out of his way? He is like a knight unhorsed—or, shall we say, deprived of his pages and trumpeters—and there are few things to compare with the arrogance and disdain with which the pedestrians treat his predicament. For it is beneath the dignity of an Italian, or a pair of Italians, afoot, to pay more than the most negligent attention to the ton or so of motor and metal nudging them from the rear. The street, after all, is theirs, and a half- or even a quarter-turn of the head is the most any man of spirit offers to the challenge. Then, their heads nodding amicably, their hands clasped behind their backs or gesticulating, the ambling conversation continues just long enough to underline their command of the situation—when, at last, unhurriedly, the strollers draw aside.*

There is always another group, walking, talking unconcernedly, just a little way farther on.

One of the first things the visiting motorist learns, voyaging through Italy, is that the words *Bivio* and *Caduta Massi*, printed on signs along the highway, are not the names of villages he is shortly to pass through. They mean, respectively, that a road intersection lies ahead and that he is entering a fallen-rock zone. A little later, he discovers that if, on stopping to ask directions, he is greeted with a swinging wave of the arm pointing straight down the roadway and a hearty "Sempre diritto," he will be well advised to get out his road map and check up, or else stop at the next intersection to inquire further.

He should learn too that his informant (if such is the

---

* The strain on the motorist in such a situation is, understandably, terrific, for the motorist is, almost by definition, in a hurry, and the pedestrian, in Italy, is not. Once, walking in Rome in the late afternoon, in the Trastevere, I saw a man break under the strain. He was large and corpulent, and both characteristics were accentuated by the fact that he was driving one of the tiny Fiat two-seaters. He was heading out from the center of the city, which meant that he had already negotiated the rush-hour traffic of the Piazza Venezia, which is enough to unman anyone. He was starting into the tangle of trolley cars, buses, motorcars and old ladies carrying shopping bags which make the Trastevere quarter so interesting, when something snapped in his mind. I was there, a pedestrian at the moment, one among the others rambling in the street in front of him, and I don't know what motivated him, whether the lights had changed while we were still in the streetway, or what. All I know is that he—obviously a man pushed beyond all endurance—gave a shriek, took his hands off the wheel and waving them wildly, pushed hard down on the accelerator and charged straight at us. We scattered, just in time.

proper term for him), however inexact his advice is, is not
really trying to mislead him. As I read the man's mind, it is
rather that, feeling cheerful himself, he wants you to feel cheerful too. Why, then, bother you with confusing talk about an
underpass here or an overpass there that you must negotiate,
the semàforo you have to turn sharp left at if you don't want
to wind up heading back towards Viterbo, and all the other
complications you'll be mixed up in soon enough, farther on?
The main thing now is to see you happily on your way.

The final lesson is a bit more complicated. I've observed
that there is an odd time-distance factor involved in most
people's feelings about the ceremony of "locking the car." In
the region where I live most of the year, in upstate New York,
for instance, I find that when I'm in my own town of Old
Chatham, or even in the nearby shopping center of Chatham,
I almost never lock the car on leaving it.

Oh, if I were going to be away all night, I might. You can
try people just so far. But otherwise I assume that Chatham
people, being neighbors, are honest, and it would take a long
time for them to overcome their principles. In the town of
Hudson, a little farther away, I am not so confident. There,
I'll leave the car for an hour or so, perhaps, but beyond that
the Hudson inhabitants are not to be trusted. I lock up.
Across the state line, in places like Pittsfield or Stockbridge—
well, you know what these Massachusetts people are like: I'd
be a fool not to lock up solidly right at the start.

This relation between home folks and strangers is sharp-
ened mightily, of course, in a foreign land. I first observed it
operating in myself when we stopped over for a few hours in
Perugia. I'd been locking the car everywhere, automatically,
till then. But this time somehow I forgot, and it was not till
we were well away from it, walking about at random, that I
remembered.

To be sure, I had parked it in a fairly busy and populous

area, and anyone taking anything from it would be almost certain to be noticed. For the matter of that, there wasn't much that was valuable in it to *be* taken. But then, who could tell what might not appeal to an Italian; and as for the thief being noticed—weren't they all in cahoots about robbing us foreigners, anyway? I realized then that any sightseeing I was going to do from then on would be done through a haze of apprehension as long as the car stayed vulnerable, and I lost no time hurrying back, keys in hand, to take proper precautions.

I sensed even then, I think, that I was being a bit foolish. But it wasn't until we reached Monteriggione that I resolved the problem. As I've said before, Monteriggione, for all its former magnificence, is now a poor and rather forsaken, rustic place. The main piazza is as big, bare and treeless as a paradeground, and when we arrived there were about eight or ten people visible, old men mostly, except for a couple of younger fellows working on a farm truck in front of a small garage.

We parked there, for a look around, and I had the car keys in my hand when I saw a couple of the old men looking at me, and somehow—though their look, I'm sure, was not really reproachful—a sense of the absurdity of what I was doing came over me.

We had said "Buon' giorno" to them, and they had nodded on their part and replied in kind. And here I was, in a town as innocently rural as my own town of Old Chatham, preparing to run about from car door to car door, turning up windows, locking, locking.

I put the keys back in my pocket and walked away—and from the feeling of ease and unworriedness that came over me I think I can safely propound a law, Coates's Law for Tourists in Italy: When you get so you don't lock up your car in a hill town you are about as much at home in the country as a tourist is ever likely to be.